"I'VE FORGOTTEN EVERYTHING I LEARNED IN SCHOOL!"

Also by Marilyn vos Savant

Ask Marilyn (1992)
The World's Most Famous Math Problem (1993)

"I'VE FORGOTTEN EVERYTHING I LEARNED IN SCHOOL!"

A Refresher Course to Help You Reclaim Your Education

Marilyn vos Savant

St. Martin's Griffin ❧ New York

Production editor: David Stanford Burr

Design: Richard Oriolo

Library of Congress Cataloging-in-Publication Data
Vos Savant, Marilyn Mach.
    "I've forgotten everything I learned in school!" / Marilyn vos
    Savant.
        p.   cm.
    ISBN 0-312-13089-9
    1. Self-culture.   2. Thought and thinking—Study and teaching.
    I. Title.
    LC32.V67   1995
    371.3'943—dc20   95-7936
                                                          CIP

First St. Martin's Griffin Edition: June 1995

10 9 8 7 6 5 4 3 2 1

Contents

Acknowledgments

A special acknowledgment goes to Richard Romano, my own guy Friday, who did all of the research for this book, which has been considerable. He kept a sharp eye out for errors, and taught me the value of a really bad joke. Moreover, he typed a large portion of the first draft with two fingers! (Well, sometimes three.) Hmm. Maybe that's why he kept asking to be paid by the hour.

And the credit for ruining centuries of the most spendid works of art known to mankind goes entirely to Nat Estes. We're much too modest to claim that *we* had anything to do with it.

Foreword

You know, sometimes I think I've forgotten everything I learned in school!" Who hasn't said this at one time or another? (And *thought* it even more often!) It's surely one of the most common complaints about how our minds do or do not work and reflects the shortcomings of just about anyone's education.

More so than even ten years ago, life is becoming increasingly competitive, a situation that is aggravated by our highly-computerized and information-driven society. It isn't easy to keep up. And think of all the things you might want to do, but don't, because you don't feel you're up to the challenge, such as starting your own business or becoming a more active participant at social gatherings. A very important part of an education is not merely the acquisition of knowledge, but the gaining of self-confidence. After all, isn't it self-confidence that's *really* the key to success? And who wouldn't feel more self-confident with better thinking skills? Add knowledge as another ingredient, and you've got the recipe for success.

Well, that makes sense, you might say, but don't I have to be intelligent enough in the first place? Don't worry. You are. Most people are far more intelligent than they think.

Intelligence is one of the most intriguing mysteries of life. None of us is quite sure how we got it or how much we have or exactly what it is, really. But emotions swirl around it even more fiercely than they do around the subject of money. And like money, most of us have an average amount, some of us have a lot, and some of us have very little. There's one thing for certain, however. We all want more.

And here's what stops too many of us. Despite the fact that we're born with a particular bone structure, most of us believe that we can make ourselves far more attractive with such deceptively simple aids as good hairstyling, well-tailored clothing, and a charming manner. And it's true, of course. After all, who was sexier? Clark Gable or Humphrey Bogart? Vivian Leigh or Bette Davis? It's impossible to say.

And although we surely inherit our body structure, we know that we can enhance its appeal and potential for good health by exercising vigorously and regularly. While Linda Hamilton and Raquel Welch may have little else in common, they both have beautiful bodies, and they didn't get them by winning a gene-pool lottery. Raquel is an exercise expert, and Linda turned a fine figure into a hard one just for a movie.

And what about money? Well, we know that's inherited, too! And we may envy other people's money just as much as we envy their nice eyes, but we also know something else. We know we don't have to settle for what we started with. We can work hard or work smart or whatever it takes, and we can make a difference in what we have. A *big* difference.

But somewhere, somehow, people have gotten the notion that they're just *stuck* with their intelligence. Well, that's like saying that we're stuck with our looks. Yes, we're stuck with them as a starting point, all right, just as we're stuck with our bodies, but why give up on self-improvement so easily? What would we look like and where would we be if we said, "Because I wasn't *born* attractive or strong or wealthy, I suppose I shouldn't try to dress well or exercise regularly or work hard." Or, "Because I've forgotten everything I learned in school, I suppose I shouldn't even *try* to improve my mind." Well, we *can* do it, we *should* do it, and here's why.

A good mind, like a work of art, is a thing of beauty. It's what lifts us beyond the ordinary—good-looking or not, stalwart or not—and makes the poet more desirable than the prince. And that's because a good mind can fascinate, enchant, captivate. When we look back in history at civilization's greatest artists and writers and statesmen, we wish we could see those people, meet those people, live with those people, *be* them.

But not because of their looks or how they were built! Who gives a hoot about how many sit-ups Mozart could do? It's his *mind* that beguiles. If we had a chance to go back to eighteenth-century Vienna and choose between one of Mozart's next-door neighbors who was in perfect physical condition or Mozart himself, who would we choose? It's not that our bodies aren't so important; it's that our minds *are.*

Even advertising and media have recognized the fact. *ABC World News* wants us to watch its program, so they advertise, "Look at the News with More Intelligence" over Peter Jennings' photograph at bus stops and on street corners. A *Fortune* magazine cover story is headlined, "Brain Power: How Intellectual Capital Is Becoming America's Most Valuable Asset." Congress declares the nineties the "Decade of the Brain." Screen actresses who once were content to be known for their looks alone now regard that as the height of professional insult. In short, it used to be smart to be attractive. But those days are long gone, and good riddance to them. In the nineties, it's attractive to be *smart.*

Even more important, mental attraction, unlike physical attraction, not only lasts, it also increases with time. When we pass our twenties or thirties or forties, and we think we don't look quite as good as we used to look, wouldn't it be great to be brighter than we ever were? After all, which holds the longest, most powerful appeal? A man's face or his mind? A woman's body or her brain?

But before beginning the program soon to follow, you should know what to expect of this book—in which you've invested hard-earned money—and what not to expect. *"I've Forgotten Everything I Learned in School!"* does not consist of pop psychology, which all too often means an author's well-meaning efforts at making his or her own personal plan succeed—at least in popularity, if not in fact. The book you're holding contains no author's wishful thinking. Instead, it's composed entirely of chapters that work with the abilities and skills that are most widely considered by authorities in the field of psychometrics to be essential indicators of a person's intelligence. These skills are tested for in school, work, government, and the armed forces.

But this book won't be coaching anyone to perform better on these tests. That would be too small a goal. Instead, the aim is to help you perform better in life. By increasing your intellectual skills and recapturing a substantial chunk of your education in the process, you can increase your chances of accomplishing that.

The Book's Structure and How to Use It

Each half of a chapter, or Book, starts with a quiz to determine how you stand with regard to the subject at hand. The purpose of the quiz is to discover your weaknesses and strengths, with the main goal being to learn more about yourself. Next, you'll find a group of exercises that specifically work on building up that skill—beginning with easy ones and ending with less easy ones (sometimes *much* less!). You should tackle at least one entire group of exercises in a single session, making note of your score and timing how long you spend on them from beginning to end. But don't worry about how long it takes. These are exercises, not tests, and you should take as much time as you need to complete them before going on. (One of the reasons that you didn't retain as much of your schooling as you'd like was the emphasis on "cramming" and "passing" instead of "learning." Well, you can leave that emphasis back in the past where it belongs. The aim of this book is to improve your mind, and there are no grades to worry about.) Still, as with physical exercise, mental exercise isn't always easy. If it were, there wouldn't be much progress.

The exercises are followed by suggestions on how you can improve in the particular skill discussed. Some suggestions will work for you and some won't, so use the ones that suit you. Also feel free to adopt any variations that come to mind. You're the one who knows yourself best, so you shouldn't hesitate to be creative. But don't stop there for the day. While the subject is fresh in your mind, move on to the second group of exercises, again beginning with easier ones and ending with more difficult ones. Score and time yourself again. If your score is higher than for the first group of exercises, and your time is lower, congratulations! You're increasing your brain power. The second half of the chapter will proceed in much the same way, exploring another aspect of the same skill.

Remember—you're not being tested. So relax and enjoy the

exercises the way people enjoy crossword puzzles. The idea is to take as long as necessary to get what you think is the answer (or give up). The time to put the book down for the evening is between chapters or chapter halves. One full chapter a day is ideal, but if you've got more ambition than patience, no one will try to stop you! Where you can measure your progress, do. It'll give you an idea of how you're improving.

The exercises are designed to build your knowledge base, as well as your skills. Instead of using the standard nonsense examples, these exercises are filled with real information about subjects with which everyone should be familiar. Gaining increased comfort with these important subjects can give you the confidence you need to pursue any of them in greater depth—or just to relax a little more at the next cocktail party you attend.

There'll be information about literature, art history, philosophy, economics, psychology, world history, religion, politics, science, film, and music—in other words, much of the material to which you were exposed in school and have nearly forgotten. But don't worry! It's much easier the second time around. And besides, you're not going to study it. Instead, it will just pass by in the course of the exercises and, without even trying, you'll pick up lost concepts and missing facts here and there to fill in gaps in your knowledge. You might even surprise yourself by finding entire new areas that interest you, or at least that look a little less forbidding than they did before.

The whole point is to absorb the knowledge painlessly, and without trying too hard, by doing exercises with solid information that you can really use. That way, the author can be confident that you're going to finish this book better than you started, one way or another.

Good luck! (But I don't really think you'll need it.)

Marilyn vos Savant

Marilyn vos Savant
New York, New York

Part One

MEMORY

BOOK ONE

Memory
Sentences and Ideas

Is your memory normal? Here's a true/false quiz.

1. Sometimes I think I've forgotten everything I learned in school except for the information and skills I use at work.
2. And if you asked me what I read in the newspaper just yesterday, I couldn't tell you much more than the headlines.
3. Despite the fact that I probably read a lot of good information, I seem to retain very little of it.
4. And I would be terrified to give a talk, even about a favorite subject, without written notes.
5. I lose things like sunglasses and umbrellas by forgetting them at lunch or leaving them in a taxi.

Even if you answered "true" to all of the above, you're probably normal! Number 1 is nearly universal. And number 4 isn't a memory problem at all; it's just a fear of public speaking. You would have no problem talking that long to a friend without notes. Number 5, too, isn't a memory problem; it's minor absentmindedness. But improving number 2 and number 3 would be of real benefit to you.

(And if you answered "false" to them all, write to me, will you? Everyone I know will want to hire you.)

Give your memory a workout with the following exercises, all from the subject of psychology. Take as long as necessary to do the best job you can. Read the paragraph once (without actually studying it), and then write down a brief reply to the questions, but without referring back to the text at all. Remember: This is a memory exercise. The answers appear at the end of these exercises on the following page.

These are known as the "transference" neuroses:

HYSTERIA is a condition in which an anxiety state is so severe that it expresses itself in a sensory loss (such as blindness) or in paralysis (such as an inability to walk).

OBSESSION is a disorder in which frustrated energy, usually thought to be sexual, is converted into repetitive, generally useless activity like constant hand-washing.

PHOBIA is a condition in which an anxiety state is deflected onto a certain object or type of situation, such as a fear of cats or a fear of heights.

And these are the questions:

1. In hysteria, what kind of state is being expressed?
2. With obsession, what kind of sexual energy is converted?
3. In phobias, what kind of state is being deflected?

These are known as the "narcissistic" neuroses:

DEMENTIA PRAECOX is the disorder now known as schizophrenia, characterized by severe disturbances in an individual's relating to the outside world.

MELANCHOLIA is the condition of being profoundly depressed, regardless of whether it is also accompanied by a manic phase.

PARANOIA is a projection of blame that has been blown out of proportion to the point of delusion, resulting in disturbances in an individual's sense of identity or personal security.

Here are a few more questions:

4. What's the original name for schizophrenia?
5. What's the original name for depression?
6. In paranoia, what has been blown out of proportion?

And here are the answers: (1) an anxiety state, (2) frustrated sexual energy, (3) again, an anxiety state, (4) dementia praecox, (5) melancholia, and (6) a projection of blame.

How did you do? Give yourself a point for each correct answer. One to two correct is probably average, three to four is pretty good, and five to six is excellent. A low score is average, because people tend to notice what they already know instead of paying attention to new information. So when we read an article about a familiar subject, we often remember only what we already knew, because we skimmed over the areas that were new to us, the way we skip unfamiliar words.

For the most attentive of you out there, here are two questions for "extra credit":

What were the "transference" neuroses we mentioned?
And what were the "narcissistic" neuroses we mentioned?
(And it's not fair if you're currently in therapy!)

Remembering Sentences and Ideas

We can think of memory as a three-stage process. First, we see or hear the new information; second, we organize it mentally; and third, we recall it when we need or want it. Strengthening any of these stages will aid in remembering information, but the following suggestions for remembering sentences and ideas will be different from the ones for remembering numbers and names, and this is why.

When remembering sentences and ideas, you're working with concepts that are recognizable to you, words that literally mean something and ideas that have some relevance to the real world. That is, they make sense. But numbers and names have no such relevance. There's no reason at all to connect a particular address with where a friend lives, and there's nothing about a stranger's looks that will give you a clue about his or her name. It's like learning a foreign language.

But let's concern ourselves with remembering facts and ideas for the moment. Make sure you absorb the information in the first place. Sit in the front of a lecture room, or lean over the table at lunch closer to the person speaking. Even if they are speaking at a normal rate, ask them to repeat themselves a couple of times, as though you hadn't quite heard them. It will tend to make them slow down overall, which is helpful in itself. And when people say less, they tend to concentrate on the more meaningful information. Later, ask them what are the most important things to remember about what they just said. They're in the best position to know, and you get the benefit of a brief summarization and repetition.

But let's say you're reading material you want to remember, instead of hearing it. Be sure to eliminate all distractions, even if you think you need them for "company." The television is the worst offender, radio is still bad, and even other people should be avoided unless they are also occupied with something and are quiet, too.

Then, remember how you were told back in school that you shouldn't read each word separately, but instead allow your eyes to scan the lines as a whole? That's because it's more difficult to make sense of words individually. So memory is improved when you don't concentrate too hard and instead allow yourself to absorb the sense of it all. In other words, take a mental *impression*.

Another good way to remember entire passages is to focus only on key words. To learn how, try to relax and allow the words to float by, while you lock onto only the most pertinent of them. You can even make notes that way, if possible.

One of the best memory aids of all, however, is to read the same information twice rapidly rather than once slowly. Repetition is the most important element in memorizing. But remember that you don't have to spend more time doing it. Read it twice—but read it twice as fast.

What about when it's necessary to remember a statement nearly verbatim? Here's a good way to do it: Close your eyes and write each word on an imaginary chalkboard, as if an instructor were writing it there for you. Before opening your eyes, "read" it once. Then open your eyes and "read" it again immediately.

Here are more exercises:

These are some of the most common "defense mechanisms":

DENIAL is the complete rejection of reality or specific aspects of reality, and can cause a retreat into a fantasy life.

DISPLACEMENT is the transfer of angry emotion from a "dangerous" object (such as a person who can retaliate) to a less dangerous one (like the cat).

INTELLECTUALIZATION is rationalization that is sometimes employed in an effort to avoid confronting a problem.

ISOLATION is how rationalization is described when it's employed in a disconnected, almost unfeeling manner.

PROJECTION is emotion that is attributed to another person, instead of the person feeling it.

Now try these questions. Answers are on the next page.

1. Denial is the complete rejection of _____.
2. Displacement is the transfer of an _____ emotion.
3. _____ is sometimes employed in an effort to avoid confronting a problem.
4. _____ is how rationalization is described when it is performed in a disconnected, almost unfeeling manner.
5. Projection is _____ that is attributed to another.

Here are a few more exercises:

These are the rest of the most common defense mechanisms:

REACTION FORMATION occurs when the sufferer convinces himself that he feels the opposite of his most dreadful feelings.

REGRESSION involves the retreat to a younger, less threatening age of development, sometimes even childhood.

REPRESSION is, simply put, a powerful forgetting of something perceived as "painful," and it's among the strongest of defense mechanisms.

REVERSAL causes the sufferer to feel that he has traded feelings with the object of his emotions.

SUBLIMATION is supposedly the energy behind much of artistic creativity. (Redirecting one's emotions into useful work makes neurosis seem almost desirable!)

And a few more questions:

6. In reaction formation, the sufferer convinces himself that he feels the _____ of his most dreadful feelings.
7. Regression involves _____ to a younger, less threatening age of development, sometimes even childhood.
8. Repression is _____ something perceived as painful.
9. Reversal causes the sufferer to feel that he has traded _____ with the object of his emotions.
10. Sublimation is said to be the energy behind _____.

Here are the answers to them all: (1) reality, (2) angry, (3) intellectualization or rationalization, (4) isolation, (5) emotion, (6) opposite, (7)
retreating, (8) forgetting, (9) feelings, and (10) creativity.

How did you do this time? If your score was about twice as high as
earlier in this chapter, you're improving. True, there were almost twice
as many exercises, but they were much harder. More important, did you
feel you improved?

In learning to improve memory, there are only three truly important factors, which I'll call the three R's:
(1) Repetition,
(2) Repetition, and
(3) Repetition!
Much of what we consider memory loss actually stems from a
failure to absorb the information in the first place. That's why the
first step to a better memory is to learn to "tune in" more than
ever before, by making a conscious decision to do so ahead of
time. The next step is to have some sort of method of noting
important information as it's seen or heard—the less complicated
the method, the better.

But there's no substitution for repetition. Repeat the information once immediately, again five minutes later, and again thirty
minutes later, and you've probably absorbed it. That may seem
hard to do at first, and you'll probably fail the first few times you
try it, but it gets easier to do as time goes on.

Also keep in mind that the more you know about a subject, the
easier it is to memorize anything about it. That's because as you
understand more of the method behind the madness, it all seems
less like trying to learn Russian. So if you've just gone back to
school—whether after a summer or a decade—and it seems as
though your brain has blown all its fuses and your forehead flashes
"TILT", hanging on long enough will help do the trick. I've felt
the same way myself.

Memory

Numbers and Names

How many of the statements below apply to you?

1. I have to repeat a telephone number over and over until I dial it, or I forget it completely.
2. If I arrive at the supermarket and discover I've forgotten to bring my grocery list, I feel almost helpless.
3. I don't know the numbers on my credit cards.
4. And I'm not positive I know my social security number.
5. And I'm always forgetting names I need to know!

Before you conclude that you're a hopeless case, consider this.

Regarding number 1, it's not normal to be able to remember telephone numbers, and it's not important, anyway. And number 2 is just a feeling, not a memory problem. When you start walking up and down the aisles, you'll probably buy nearly everything you need. As for number 3, the people who know their credit-card numbers are usually just the ones who shop by telephone, not the ones with a better memory. But if number 4 is true, make learning your social security number your first exercise. And if number 5 is true, too, you should work on that problem.

In short, you may need a little improvement, but not nearly as much as you might have thought.

Here are some exercises:

The following people are among the most famous in psychiatry and psychology:

ALFRED ADLER was the psychiatrist who introduced the term "inferiority feeling," later known, often incorrectly, as "inferiority complex."
SIGMUND FREUD was the psychiatrist known widely as the father of psychoanalysis, who insisted that neurosis had sexual bases.
CARL JUNG was the psychiatrist who developed the concepts of extroversion, introversion, and the collective unconscious.
IVAN PAVLOV was the physiologist who introduced the concept of the conditioned reflex, most famously in the case where he trained a dog to salivate at the sound of a bell.
B. F. SKINNER was the psychologist who was an outspoken proponent of behaviorism, best known for his Skinner box, in which animal behavior was observed.

And here are a few questions:

1. Who introduced the term "inferiority feeling"?
2. Who insisted that neurosis had sexual bases?
3. Who developed the concept of the collective unconscious?
4. Who introduced the concept of the conditioned reflex?
5. Who was an outspoken proponent of behaviorism?

That was terrible, wasn't it? Let's try it again. (And don't believe anyone who says psychology is an easy subject.)
This time, go back and reread each paragraph, but ignore the first name. Instead, try to imprint just the last name and connect only a couple of words from the paragraph with it.

Here are the questions again:

1. Who introduced the term "inferiority feeling"?
2. Who insisted that neurosis had sexual bases?
3. Who developed the concept of the collective unconscious?
4. Who introduced the concept of the conditioned reflex?
5. Who was an outspoken proponent of behaviorism?

Psychiatry and psychology aren't the easiest subjects in the world, but they aren't the toughest, either, and difficulty with the above exercises doesn't have anything to do with your intelligence. Rather, it has more to do with acquiring a little more skill with memory and overcoming the intimidation so many of us feel in connection with it.

Here are the answers: Give yourself a separate score for the first time you did the exercises and the second time. (1) Adler, (2) Freud, (3) Jung, (4) Pavlov, and (5) Skinner.

An average score the first time is one to two; good is three to four; superior is five. Although the names may have been familiar to you, we purposely didn't ask about common information, because this is not a test in psychology. These are memory exercises.

Did you improve the second time? If nothing else, that shows the value of repetition and/or paying attention to the most relevant information. (And you clearly learned something as well.)

Remembering Numbers and Names

Actually, remembering numbers and names is *harder* than learning a foreign language. At least many of the foreign languages we study have a lot in common with our own. We could travel to France or Spain or Italy, for example, and actually read many of the words we see. But remember the phrase, "It's Greek to me!"? Well, with numbers and names, that's how it is to us, all right! After all, which of the following is the easier to remember?

1-7-15-18-7-5-15-21-19-13-1-14-9-19-19-9-20-20-9-14-7-15-14-25 15-21-18-19-15-6-1-9-14-5-9-19-21-14-4-5-18-19-8-9-18-20

or

A GORGEOUS MAN IS SITTING ON YOUR SOFA IN HIS UNDERSHIRT

The top lines, as you've probably guessed, contain the same amount of numbers as the bottom lines have letters, but because we don't "read" with numbers, they're meaningless to us. If we *did* read with them, we'd immediately see that they stand for the letters of the alphabet and read the same as the bottom lines.

Personally, I don't bother with memorizing numbers and names unless the answer is "yes" to at least one of these questions:

1. Will I need to know this particular information again, and if so, will it be difficult to locate?

2. Will I look foolish if I don't remember this information at some point in the future?

I memorize those few numbers that I *do* need, by writing them down, transferring them to a telephone directory myself, and then not referring to it again until after I've made my best guess. If I'm wrong, I correct myself, and then try again next time. The best way I've found to *forget* a name and number is to open my address book every time I pick up the telephone or write a letter. Why, I put my son's and daughter's numbers at school on my speed dial, and I didn't remember them even a *year* later.

If you're game for a more creative technique, you might be able to handle mnemonics. The best (and silliest) book I know on the subject is *Remembrance of Things Fast* by Susan Ferraro, who answers the question, "What makes a good mnemonic?" with the reply, "Sex, slander, and sixth-grade humor."

Some people visualize, but others use all sorts of verbal devices such as acronyms, epigrams, and rhymes. Here's one of my own— a way to remember the order and names of the planets:

"My verdant earth must journey as a star unites nine planets."

My (Mercury)
   Verdant (Venus)
      Earth (Earth)
         Must (Mars)
            Journey (Jupiter)
              as a
                 Star (Saturn)
                    Unites (Uranus)
                       Nine (Neptune)
                         Planets (Pluto)

Now it's time for more exercises:

These are probably the most well-known psychological therapies:
PSYCHOANALYSIS is the oldest method for treating emotional disorders and emphasizes the unconscious as the most important basis of them.
PSYCHOTHERAPY treats mental disorders by establishing a personal, often emotional, relationship between a trained clinician and the sufferer.

BEHAVIOR THERAPY is more direct, and it attempts to alter behavior with conditioning techniques, such as rewards and reinforcements.

COGNITIVE THERAPY is also a direct approach, but it uses conditioning techniques to attempt to alter thoughts and feelings.

GESTALT. Ah, but we couldn't leave you without modern Gestalt, which simply tries to get you to say what you actually feel instead of saying what you actually say (Really.)

And here are the questions:

1. What is the name of the oldest method for treating emotional disorders and that emphasizes the unconscious?
2. What is the name of the therapy that treats mental disorders by establishing a personal relationship?
3. What is the name of the therapy that attempts to alter behavior with conditioning techniques?
4. What is the name of the therapy that uses conditioning techniques to attempt to alter thoughts and feelings?
5. And what is the modern therapy that simply tries to get you to say what you actually feel?

We hope that felt a little better. And we also hope that you found a shortcut or trick of your own here and there, such as deleting the word "therapy" as you deleted the first names. Getting rid of clutter makes the whole process of memorization far easier. For example, just deleting the middle initial from your business card makes it easier for people to remember your name.

Here are the answers: (1) psychoanalysis, (2) psychotherapy, (3) behavior therapy, (4) cognitive therapy, and (5) Gestalt.

How did you do? Anything over three is very good.

But remember what we said about repetition? Try these one last time. (The answers follow directly, so cover them up now.)

1. Who introduced the term "inferiority feeling"?
2. Who insisted that neurosis had sexual bases?
3. Who developed the concept of the collective unconscious?
4. Who introduced the concept of the conditioned reflex?
5. Who was an outspoken proponent of behaviorism?

And here are the answers: (1) Adler, (2) Freud, (3) Jung, (4) Pavlov, and (5) Skinner.

Did you improve again? If so, you're probably acquiring the basic skills, and just practicing a little every day will make them easier to use each time.

Our memories are enormously powerful intellectual tools, and there has been a wealth of information published about the subject. But my personal assessment is that memory isn't all that important to intellectual functioning. Most of the memory systems I've investigated are laborious to learn, agonizing actually to implement, and are probably not much more than a fanciful substitute for simply writing down a little list and putting it in your pocket.

In other words, I think we should exercise our memories to aid in comprehension, and use a little trick or two to help us remember the occasional important name, but not worry about it much beyond that. There's too much relevant information in our lives for any one person to keep it all in his or her head.

Some psychologists maintain that we never actually "forget" anything, and that our brains are more like computers than we know, storing up all sorts of valuable and worthless information, like old toys and hats in the attic. This is meant to be a positive state of affairs, of course, but considering a few of the dreams I've had over the years, I wonder if it might not be so bad to cultivate the art of forgetting.

Imagine. We could forget all the ghastly episodes that occurred after proms, the humiliation of our first job, and even delete entire embarrassing relationships. Of course, this would be devastating to the incomes of psychiatrists and psychologists all over the country, but nothing's perfect, is it?

BOOK TWO

General Literacy
Common Knowledge

Do you have enough "common knowledge"? Here's a true/false quiz to help you find out:

1. I find myself avoiding conversations with knowledge-able people and often miss social and business contacts as a result.
2. And if I find myself stuck talking with them, I usually try to make it brief. Unless they're good-looking, that is.
3. Regardless, I seem to manage to bluff my way through most gatherings somehow, even if I have to spend a lot of time eating.
4. I can hold my own in most conversations as long as they don't last more than twenty minutes.
5. And if it's longer than that, I always turn the conversation to social issues.

Answering "true" to number 1 and number 2 shows you're lacking in self-confidence. A little more basic knowledge could do wonders for you. "Trues" to number 3 and number 4 are normal, even if not exactly what you'd prefer. And a "true" to number 5 is a sure sign that you've got plenty of conversational ability and self-confidence, but not enough common knowledge about this fascinating world and the way it works.

Bolster your common knowledge with the following exercises, all from the subject of great literature. As we move backward through the literary history of the Western world, read slowly through each group of titles and authors, then do the short matching exercise that follows.

Here are three twentieth-century novels:

Remembrance of Things Past by Marcel Proust (1927)
   (Now commonly called *In Search of Lost Time*)
The Magic Mountain by Thomas Mann (1924)
Ulysses by James Joyce (1922)

Without looking up, match column A to column B:

A	B
1. James Joyce	*Remembrance of Things Past*
2. Thomas Mann	*The Magic Mountain*
3. Marcel Proust	*Ulysses*

Here are four nineteenth-century novels:

War and Peace by Leo Tolstoy (1869)
Crime and Punishment by Fyodor Dostoevsky (1866)
Madame Bovary by Gustave Flaubert (1856)
Moby-Dick by Herman Melville (1851)

Again, without looking up, match column A to column B:

A	B
4. Fyodor Dostoevsky	*War and Peace*
5. Gustave Flaubert	*Crime and Punishment*
6. Herman Melville	*Madame Bovary*
7. Leo Tolstoy	*Moby-Dick*

Here are three nineteenth-century English novels:

Wuthering Heights by Emily Brontë (1847)
Jane Eyre by Charlotte Brontë (1847)
Emma by Jane Austen (1816)

And you know what to do next, of course:

A	B
8. Jane Austen	*Jane Eyre*
9. Charlotte Brontë	*Wuthering Heights*
10. Emily Brontë	*Emma*

Here are the answers: (1) *Ulysses,* (2) *The Magic Mountain,* (3) *Remembrance of Things Past,* (4) *Crime and Punishment,* (5) *Madame Bovary,* (6) *Moby-Dick,* (7) *War and Peace,* (8) *Emma,* (9) *Jane Eyre,* and (10) *Wuthering Heights.*

How was that for a start? Not bad, I'll bet. Most people know quite a bit more than they think they do, and they just need a little help getting familiar with the material again. You probably felt certain of no more than a few of the names when you started. Still, nearly all were familiar to you somehow. You knew they were authors, not composers, for example, but depending on how long you've been out of school, you probably were vague on the rest.

It's not surprising. Many of us have our educations forced upon us at a very young age, then turn our backs on learning forever. And even if we don't want that to be the case, we can't seem to find the time to do anything about it.

Common Knowledge

One of the best ways to acquire "common knowledge" is through reading, and fiction is particularly useful. Nonfiction is fine, of course, but it's usually more specialized, and we're aiming for a broader base here. And you not only learn about life, you also can discuss it with others. One of the most pleasurable learning experiences I know is to read a good book with a fine friend or loved one. Whether you do it alone or together, what happens afterward can be an affair to remember, all right. Talking over pizza at midnight or over coffee at dawn, it's amazing how your own world can retreat into perspective, your worries becoming less important and your satisfactions more poignant.

And if you're alone, exploring the world of literature can be as intensely pleasurable as traveling alone, although just as fearsome at first. Picking up a great novel can feel like stepping out of a taxi in Shanghai. Everyone seems to know his way around but you. The currency in your pocket looks like play money. The menus in windows are filled with what looks like scribbles and scratches.

So you sit down on a bench and look around. A child trips over your shoe and giggles. A paper dragon is caught in a tree. The air is alive with the tinkling of bells. And there you are, alone with your consciousness, the only one in the world in that few square feet, and it's delicious. And so it is with a good book. It's just you there, in your corner of the world, and nothing else matters. You'll see.

But in addition to their more sensual satisfactions, books are a source of "common knowledge," and this method of acquisition is utterly painless. Here is an important suggestion. Go out and buy yourself a fine-quality modern novel that takes place "in another world." Let's say you're from a small town or medium-sized city. Try *Bonfire of The Vanities* by Tom Wolfe, written in 1987. The book is set in New York City and filled with absorbing facts about big-city life. Or maybe you're an accountant. How about trying *The Pale Horse* by Agatha Christie, written in 1962, or one of her many other fine detective stories? You'll learn about everything from plants to poison. Yes, you could go out and buy yourself a botany textbook, but would it be anywhere near as much fun? And botany textbooks are restricted to botany. What about all the other facts that Agatha Christie will take you to visit?

Once you've spent some months getting back into shape with modern authors, the classics may become irresistible. But don't start with them. Plainly put, they're just too difficult. Picking up a copy of *Ulysses* or *Remembrance of Things Past* if you haven't read anything challenging for a while will make your brain feel something like the way that your legs feel after your first skiing trip of the season. Bad. You need practice for these gems.

But what about the middle of the season? There you are, zooming contentedly down the intermediate slopes, falling only once or twice. You look up at the expert trails, and your heart pounds with excitement. Could you do it? Bet you can.

Here are a lot of titles by only two authors, but you should know them, if not by heart, then by ear.

These novels were written by Charles Dickens:

Oliver Twist (1838), *Nicholas Nickleby* (1839), *The Old Curiosity Shop* (1841), *Barnaby Rudge* (1841), *Dombey and Son* (1848), *David Copper-*

field (1850), *Bleak House* (1853), *Hard Times* (1854), *Little Dorrit* (1857), *A Tale of Two Cities* (1859), *Great Expectations* (1861), *Our Mutual Friend* (1865), and *The Mystery of Edwin Drood* (1870; unfinished).

And these plays were written (years are approximate) by the incomparable literary genius William Shakespeare.

Histories:
Henry VI, Parts I, II, and III (1590), *Richard III* (1592), *Richard II* (1594), *King John* (1596), *Henry IV, Parts I* and *II* (1597), *Henry V* (1598), and *Henry VIII* (1612; probably written with John Fletcher).

Comedies:
The Comedy of Errors (1592), *The Taming of the Shrew* (1593), *The Two Gentlemen of Verona* (1594), *Love's Labour's Lost* (1594), *A Midsummer Night's Dream* (1595), *The Merchant of Venice* (1596), *Much Ado About Nothing* (1598), *As You Like It* (1599), *Twelfth Night* (1599), *The Merry Wives of Windsor* (1600), *Troilus and Cressida* (1601), *All's Well That Ends Well* (1602), *Measure for Measure* (1604), and *Two Noble Kinsmen* (1612; of doubtful authorship, it may have been written with John Fletcher).

Tragedies:
Titus Andronicus (1593), *Romeo and Juliet* (1594), *Julius Caesar* (1599), *Hamlet* (1600), *Othello* (1604), *King Lear* (1605), *Macbeth* (1605), *Antony and Cleopatra* (1606), *Coriolanus* (1607), and *Timon of Athens* (1607).

Tragicomedies:
Pericles (1608), *Cymbeline* (1609), *The Winter's Tale* (1610), and *The Tempest* (1611).

Here's an exercise: Go back and read the list of books that Dickens wrote and the list of Shakespeare's plays. This is because we know you only skimmed them the first time. Actually read them this time. (It'll only take a minute or two.)

And here's another exercise: Next to each one of Shakespeare's plays in the list below (now in chronological order), guess whether it's a history (H), a comedy (C), a tragedy (T), or a tragicomedy (TC). But don't look back. This is an exercise, not a quiz.

(1) *Henry VI, Parts I, II,* and *III,* (2) *Richard III,* (3) *The Comedy of Errors,* (4) *Titus Adronicus,* (5) *The Taming of the Shrew,* (6) *The Two Gentlemen of Verona,* (7) *Love's Labour's Lost,* (8) *Romeo and Juliet,* (9) *Richard II,* (10) *A Midsummer Night's Dream,* (11) *King John,* (12) *The Merchant of Venice,* (13) *Henry IV, Parts I and II,* (14) *Much Ado About Nothing,* (15)

Henry V, (16) *Julius Caesar*, (17) *As You Like It*, (18) *Twelfth Night*, (19) *Hamlet*, (20) *The Merry Wives of Windsor*, (21) *Troilus and Cressida*, (22) *All's Well That Ends Well*, (23) *Measure for Measure*, (24) *Othello*, (25) *King Lear*, (26) *Macbeth*, (27) *Antony and Cleopatra*, (28) *Coriolanus*, (29) *Timon of Athens*, (30) *Pericles*, (31) *Cymbeline*, (32) *The Winter's Tale*, (33) *The Tempest*, (34) *Henry VIII*, and (35) *Two Noble Kinsmen*.

Here are the answers:

(1) H	(2) H	(3) C	(4) T	(5) C	(6) C	(7) C
(8) T	(9) H	(10) C	(11) H	(12) C	(13) H	(14) C
(15) H	(16) T	(17) C	(18) C	(19) T	(20) C	(21) C
(22) C	(23) C	(24) T	(25) T	(26) T	(27) T	(28) T
(29) T	(30) TC	(31) TC	(32) TC	(33) TC	(34) H	(35) C

How did you do? Thirty to thirty-five correct? I'm impressed. You weren't supposed to do that well. Twenty to thirty? Surprising, isn't it? Now you can tell most of Shakespeare's plays apart just by how the titles sound. That was good exercise. Ten to twenty? Try the exercise again. First read, then guess. Under ten? Try again tomorrow.

And here's the last set of exercises for this section:

These two titles are from the Middle Ages:

The Canterbury Tales by Geoffrey Chaucer (1400)
The Divine Comedy by Dante (1321)

And these three titles are from Ancient Greece:

Oedipus Rex by Sophocles (about 450 B.C.)
The Iliad and *The Odyssey* by Homer (9th century B.C.)

And the exercise? Just go back and read them one or two more times. You've done enough.

―――――――――――――――――――――――――――――――――――

So now you know the secret to "common knowledge." It's experience. And you can get it through the written page even better than you can in life. This is because you only have time to live one life in reality, but you can experience many other lives through books. And who knows? Maybe you'll become so fascinated with one of them that you'll change the way you're living. Maybe you'll become more outgoing. Maybe you'll decide to travel more. (But take a book along. Nicholas Byam Shaw, the chairman of London publishing house Macmillan Publishers Ltd., told me how he carried a volume of Proust with him whenever he traveled. "And when I'm forced to wait in an airport somewhere," he said, 'despite all that's going on around me, I just take out my book and enter that world. The time evaporates.")

With the classics, especially, I recommend visiting a secondhand bookshop if you like an old-fashioned atmosphere. (If not, a modern bookstore will provide you with a brighter, fresher, less-expensive copy.) Like time, my *Ulysses* had disappeared over the years, and I stopped in a nice old place in New York one misty Sunday afternoon to replace it. Before long, that and two other dusty volumes joined my armload of fresh bread, raisin rolls, and muffins. At home, however, although I intended to slide it onto my shelf, I happened to put it down on the bedroom sofa instead. Late that night, I turned on the reading light there and found that faded fifty-year-old volume of *Ulysses* in the spotlight. Everything else was dark. The entire world seemed dark. And so I sat down and opened it, hesitantly. That's all I remember.

General Literacy
Uncommon Knowledge

How do you feel about your "uncommon knowledge"? Try this true/false quiz.

1. As time goes by, I can no longer remember whether I read only the notes for a book or whether I read the book itself.
2. And I'm not even sure whether I remember it from the book or from the movie.
3. But at least I'm pretty good at trivia games.
4. Although I don't exactly astound people at parties.
5. In fact, I avoid parties and plenty of other social encounters, at least partly because the situation might expose how little I know. I'd much rather meet people in my profession, where I can feel knowledgeable.

If you answered "true" to three out of the first four statements, cheer up. You're normal. Not that you like feeling that way, but at least you're not alone. If you answered "true" to number 5, though, you're suffering from unnecessary insecurity. Everyone I know who is single moans about how difficult it is to meet people, but most of them make a point of avoiding the very social situations where they might find someone. What a waste! Read on.

Here are more exercises. First read these brief plot descriptions of the modern novels mentioned in the first half of this chapter. Then do the equally brief exercise that follows.

Remembrance of Things Past is a long novel of seven parts. As its title indicates, the narrator is "in search of lost time," and he finds the true meaning of experience in memories that are unexpectedly provoked of experiences that were unappreciated at the time.

The Magic Mountain is concerned with the personal development of a young man at a tuberculosis sanatorium in the Swiss Alps. Symbolically, it serves as a model of a decadent Europe on the brink of the First World War.

Ulysses, which had the literary advantage of being both obscure and banned in the United States until 1933, is a study of the disintegration of society through the events of an average day in the lives of its three leading characters, residents of Dublin.

Without looking back, answer the following questions:

1. What long novel explored a "search for lost time" through reminiscences?
2. What novel symbolically pondered a decadent Europe on the brink of war?
3. What novel, banned in the United States, studied the disintegration of society?

The answers are 1) *Remembrance of Things Past*, 2) *The Magic Mountain*, and 3) *Ulysses*. You may know all three plot descriptions by now. If not, just read through them one more time.

Here are the plots in brief from those nineteenth-century novels:

War and Peace focuses on the invasion of Russia by Napoleon's army in 1812 and its effect on more than five hundred characters from all levels of society throughout the preceding years and following it.

Crime and Punishment explores the mind of a poor student who believes he has committed the perfect murder until relentless guilt drives him to confession and subsequent repentance and peace.

Madame Bovary follows the life of an ordinary, tragically unfulfilled wife of a country doctor as she seeks romantic love so desperately that she amasses intolerable debts and adulterous humiliations, which ultimately lead to her suicide.

Moby-Dick chronicles a search for the great white whale of the same name by the monomaniacal Captain Ahab. A deeply symbolic examination of good and evil, it is straightforward, adventurous, and drives to the thrilling climax we all know.

Here's a little more exercise:

4. Give a one-sentence description of *War and Peace*.
5. Do the same for the plot of *Crime and Punishment*.
6. And the same for the plot of *Madame Bovary*.
7. And now do the same for the plot of *Moby-Dick*.

There are no pat answers here. You probably know how you did. And that's likely to be good and getting better.

Uncommon Knowledge

To gain from reading a classic novel, first read a good set of notes, if it exists—unless you're the sort of person who will lose interest if you know "how it will turn out." (But try not to be that kind of person! Remember this: We're all going to die, and we know it. We know "how it will turn out." But that doesn't mean we should lose interest in everything that happens before then.)

Great novels can be complex, and your appreciation can be enhanced by a little preparation. But don't make a chore of it. Just buy a set of notes, read it through without bothering to puzzle anything out, and then move on to the book. Unanswered questions will dissolve as you turn the pages.

But don't see the movie until afterward—if you do at all. The interest in a novel comes from writing technique, and the plot and characters can't be separated from how they're described and developed in words. If the movie version of a novel works, that's fine, but its success doesn't come from the success of the novel and has little to do with it. Movies are an entirely different medium, and seeing Hollywood's heavily salted or sweetened version of the plot and characters beforehand will destroy your appreciation of the real thing.

Even more important, don't ever read a condensed version of a great novel as a substitute for reading the whole book. This is like seeing *The Sound of Music* with the songs edited out. Without the author's original words, it's just another book—and a dull one, at that.

There are more ways to gain "uncommon knowledge" than from reading fiction, but I know of none easier, less expensive, and more enjoyable. Still, those other ways are there, and here are a few of them.

Take an elementary adult-education course in a subject foreign to you. If you've always been interested in art, purposely take a course in repairing common household appliances. Likewise, if you're a wizard with the toolbox, take a course in art appreciation. The idea is to purposely immerse yourself in whatever you may be avoiding. By the end of the course, you'll find your self-confidence greatly enhanced.

Another suggestion is to seek out people who are very different from you, or seemingly so. Make their acquaintance, visit their homes, and talk to them about their lives and yours, making sure that you give as much as you take, or more. By purposely leaving familiar territory, you'll not only learn a great deal, you may also get rid of whatever prejudice may have come from a simple fear of the unknown.

A third suggestion is doing a little volunteer work in your spare time. Many charitable or nonprofit organizations will be delighted to have you, and you'll have a low-pressure opportunity to explore areas that might have been otherwise inaccessible to you. You can get plenty of "uncommon knowledge" behind the scenes at your public television station or local art museum or even at the police and fire departments, if they'll have you. And you'll be doing some good at the same time

---

We haven't run out of plots, of course.

Wuthering Heights tells the stormy tale of the thwarted love affair between the strange, passionate Heathcliff and his adopted father's daughter, who marries another man. Their lives are deeply intertwined until death.

Jane Eyre is a shy, but intense orphan who works as a governess for Mr. Rochester, a moody, violent man. The terrible secret revealed on the day they are to marry is that he is already married, and to a woman who is insane.

Emma, having nothing better to do than care for her father, takes a controlling interest in other people's affairs of the heart, which eventually has great impact on her own.

And here's an exercise:

1. What is the common element in the above three novels?
2. And what are two elements their authors have in common?

Here are the answers:
1) The most obvious element these novels share is the subject of romance—whether you call it passion, love, or simply male/female relationships, and 2) all the authors are female and English.

Emily (*Wuthering Heights*) and Charlotte (*Jane Eyre*) Brontë were sisters, and are considered talented in that order. A third sister Anne, the least regarded of the three, also wrote novels.

Jane Austen (*Emma*) is often considered the greatest of all female novelists, however. She also wrote *Sense and Sensibility*, *Pride and Prejudice*, and *Mansfield Park*, among other novels.

Continuing on backward in time, here are the last of the literary plots.

The Canterbury Tales is an unfinished, poetic work that describes the stories told by some thirty very different people as they make their annual spring pilgrimage to Becket's shrine at Canterbury.

The Divine Comedy is an epic poem that takes the author on a tour of Hell, Purgatory, and Paradise. As if that weren't enough, it's all based on the teachings of St. Thomas Aquinas.

Oedipus Rex is a play about the tragic hero who unwittingly kills his biological father (who had taken him from his mother and left him to die as an infant) and later marries his natural mother. He blinds himself in remorse.

The Iliad is an epic poem of two-dozen books of dactylic hexameter verse and chronicles the events of the last few days of the Trojan War, although in mythic proportion. Controversy still continues as to whether Homer was a single poet or many.

The Odyssey is another epic poem, although it is often called the first novel. It recounts the adventures of Odysseus on his way home after the Trojan War through the weaving of folk tales and legends from other lands.

The exercise? Wasn't reading that enough? No, despite the fact that these are classics, it's unlikely that you'll ever have anything to do with them. They're far too abstruse to do you any practical good. But you should know they're there. (And if you ever feel strong enough to read them, you may be in for a pleasant surprise.)

"Uncommon knowledge" strengthens your intellect—at least partly because you can use it to understand more than what you read in the newspapers or see on the television or hear on the radio. It helps to demystify the world and can make your life a little easier. Perhaps most important, it can give you more of the confidence we all need to tolerate the barrage of daily messages from the outside world and still make up our own minds. That's rare these days.

But here's where you may be in for a surprise. While I hope you've become a little more interested in the "other words" to be had just for the price of a novel or a library card, I have another suggestion: Don't talk about what you've done.

What?! You should make the effort to read a great classic, perhaps even the seven volumes of Proust, and not even get the pleasure of pronouncing his name correctly at the next cocktail party you attend? Yes. That was never the point of all this. If you do go out and read those seven volumes, keep them "in your back pocket," so to speak. Don't use them to impress your neighbors; use them to be a more confident person, instead. Let your increased understanding of the world lift up your entire spirit.

When people are pretentious, they look smaller, not larger. And they *are* smaller. That's why they're trying so hard. Otherwise, they wouldn't need to bother. Don't you be one of them. Just be yourself.

BOOK THREE

Vocabulary

General

Do any of these statements apply to you? How many do?

1. When I'm reading, I generally skip right over words I don't know.
2. But I usually try to discover what they mean in context.
3. And I'm successful most of the time.
4. And when it's really important, I look up a word.
5. In fact, I always keep a dictionary at hand when I read.

Don't feel bad. A "true" to number 1 is perfectly normal. But a "true" to number 2 draws mixed reviews. If you answered "false" to number 3, then your "true" to number two is a good sign. But if you answered "true" to number 3, then your "true" to number 2 is a bad sign. You only get the loosest notion of what a word means by its context. If you're reading physical science, for example, and you don't know the meaning of a word, you're surely fooling yourself to guess. And if you're reading political science, you're likely to assign the meaning according to your particular school of thought. That is, it'll seem to mean whatever you want it to mean. A "true" to number 4 is an excellent sign, and a "true" to number 5 is unusual and means you sure must never read on an exercise bike!

Here are some exercises, all from the subject of economics. (And if it's convenient, start timing yourself at this point.)

Read the generic definitions of the following words. Remember that initially seeing a word alone, out of its context, can be an aid to understanding the context.

SUPPLY: The quantity on hand or available for use.
DEMAND: The act of claiming as a right.
PRODUCTION: The process of creation by mental or physical effort.
CONSUMPTION: The process of ingesting, spending, or using up.

Here are a few questions about these words. See if you sharpened your definitions:

1. SUPPLY: The quantity on hand or available for _____.
2. DEMAND: The act of claiming as a _____.
3. PRODUCTION: Creation by mental or _____ effort.
4. CONSUMPTION: Ingesting, spending, or _____.

Here are three more words:

PRODUCTIVITY: The amount of creation by mental or physical effort.
COMMODITY: An article of usefulness or value.
PROFIT: An advantage or benefit.

And here are three more questions:

5. PRODUCTIVITY: The _____ of creation by mental or physical effort.
6. COMMODITY: An _____ of usefulness or value.
7. PROFIT: An _____ or benefit.

A few more words:

UNEMPLOYMENT: The state of not being used.
UNION: The act of bringing together so as to form a whole.
LABOR: Physical or mental exertion at a task.
STRIKE: To inflict a sharp blow.

And a few more questions:

8. UNEMPLOYMENT: The state of not being _____.
9. UNION: Bringing together so as to form a _____.
10. LABOR: Physical or mental exertion at a _____.
11. STRIKE: To inflict a sharp _____.

Still more words:

INFLATION: The swelling of an object with gas or air.
RECESSION: The act of withdrawing or going back.
DEPRESSION: A place that is sunk below its surroundings.

And still more questions:

12. INFLATION: The _____ of an object with gas or air.
13. RECESSION: The act of _____ or going back.
14. DEPRESSION: A place that is _____ _____ its surroundings.

Here are the answers: (1) use, (2) right, (3) physical, (4) using up, (5) amount, (6) article, (7) advantage, (8) used, (9) whole, (10) task, (11) blow, (12) swelling, (13) withdrawing, and (14) sunk below.

How did you do? (You can stop timing temporarily.)

General Vocabulary

Even though these words were familiar to you in their common usage, the exercises should have caused you to have another look at them and add to the meanings you already knew. Take the word "strike," for example. In this generic context, we recall its more violent meaning. And the word "recession" is another good example. "Going back" to an earlier level, especially with reference to prices, might take on new meaning. (When housing prices are low, people who want to buy homes are happy, but people who want to sell them are unhappy. When interest rates are low, people who want to take out loans are delighted, but people who have money in the bank are miserable. What *is* a recession, anyway?)

As you can see, the interest here is not in how you scored, but whether there is more to the words than we think at first. In other words, the words you *don't* look up may be even more important than those you do!

Here's a suggestion. Remember the joke at the beginning of the chapter about keeping a dictionary at hand whenever you read? Well, *keep a dictionary at hand whenever you read.* No kidding. But here's the difference.

Don't look up every word you don't know. Don't even look up most of them. And don't feel guilty about it. Just acquire a good, but lightweight dictionary and get in the habit of carrying it from room to room with any book you're currently reading. I do it all the time. Think of the two of them as a cup and saucer—they go together. If you prop yourself up in bed to read, keep the book in your hands and the dictionary on the nightstand. Let it stay unopened, if you wish. But just keep it there, like a security blanket. It'll be there when you need it.

The best words to look up first are words that you think you know but are not totally, absolutely sure about. Here are a few pairs that may surprise you. Most of us think they mean generally the same thing, but they're really quite different.

AMBIGUOUS, EQUIVOCAL—An ambiguous statement is made by someone who doesn't make himself clear, but an equivocal statement is made by someone who doesn't want to be clear.

ARCHETYPE, PROTOTYPE—An archetype is the pattern that served as the model for future generations, but the prototype was only the first one.

CLIMATIC, CLIMACTIC—Climatic refers to a climate, but climactic refers to a climax.

CREDIBLE, CREDULOUS—A credible person is believable, but a credulous person is gullible.

FLAUNT, FLOUT—If a person flaunts his authority, he makes a show of it, but if a person flouts authority, he defies it.

MERETRICIOUS, MERITORIOUS—A meretricious woman resembles a prostitute, but a meritorious woman is one who deserves credit.

PRONE, SUPINE—When you're in a prone position, you're lying flat on your stomach; when you're in a supine position, you're lying flat on your back.

One interesting way to discover just how much your vocabulary needs improving is to try this: For just a week, read the entire front page of your daily newspaper very critically, circling with a ballpoint every word you're not positive you know. Don't hold back! You're not going to look them up. And if you're embarrassed or don't want to spoil the paper for anyone else, buy yourself an extra copy.

Depressing, isn't it?

A large vocabulary is more important than you might initially think. It's very difficult to talk and think about concepts for which you have no accurate words. True, there are insecure people who purposely use polysyllabic words in an effort to impress others, but that's not a laudable function of vocabulary. Aside from better communication, a larger vocabulary will enhance your intelligence. And it *can* be done. It'll take continued effort, but you've obviously got what it takes, or you wouldn't be reading this book.

And speaking of reading books, don't forget to try most any of the little vocabulary-building paperbacks available. I have no favorites, but I can make a suggestion. If you find them too much of a chore to read, just read them through as you would a novel. That is, don't agonize over every page and feel like you're back in school again. Just read them lightly—like the newspaper. You'll retain plenty, easily enough to make the price worth it.

In the next set of exercises, the terms will be increasingly peculiar ("peculiar": unique; belonging in a distinctive way) to the subject of economics, but again will be made generic for you. (Start timing again, adding this to the last time.)

LONG RUN: A condition seen over an extended period of time.
SHORT RUN: A condition seen over a brief period of time.
MACRO-: A prefix meaning large or broad.
MICRO-: A prefix meaning small or narrow.
FREE MARKET: A place where all may buy and sell.
PLANNED MARKET: A place for regulated buying and selling.

Now fill in the missing word(s):

1. **LONG RUN:** A condition seen over an _____ period.
2. **SHORT RUN:** A condition seen over a _____ period.
3. **MACRO-:** A prefix meaning large or _____.
4. **MICRO-:** A prefix meaning small or _____.
5. **FREE MARKET:** A place where _____ may buy and sell.
6. **PLANNED MARKET:** A place for _____ buying and selling.

More definitions:

GROSS NATIONAL PRODUCT: What a country produces and sells each year.
GROSS DOMESTIC PRODUCT: What a country produces and sells only within its borders each year.

CONSUMER PRICE INDEX: A measure of living costs based on changes in retail prices.

COST OF LIVING: Cost of maintaining a particular lifestyle.

And more questions:

7. GROSS NATIONAL PRODUCT: What a country produces and sells each _____.

8. GROSS DOMESTIC PRODUCT: What a country produces and sells only within its _____ each year.

9. CONSUMER PRICE INDEX: A measure of _____ _____ based on changes in retail prices.

10. COST OF LIVING: Cost of maintaining a _____ _____.

And the answers: (1) extended, (2) brief, (3) broad, (4) narrow, (5) all, (6) regulated, (7) year, (8) borders, (9) living costs, and (10) particular lifestyle.

How did you do? If you got the sense of the first eight, although not the exact words, that's excellent. The last two are more difficult to separate. (And you can stop timing now.)

But the terms consumer price index and cost of living illustrate an important point—not on the subject of economics, but in the importance of vocabulary. Here's an exercise that only involves a little reading. Dust off the kids' encyclopaedia and read the entries on those two terms. Then think about whether it's good or bad when they go up or down. It's not the black-and-white issue that your newscaster might make it seem. And that shouldn't be how we make judgments, anyway! (If she smiles, it's good news, and if she frowns, it's bad news?)

The first half of this chapter concentrated on looking at words in a generic sense—almost in a theoretical way—and one of the things you can go back and notice is that these words don't have obvious one-word synonyms. Most words don't. New words are more often added to a dynamic language because they express something *different*. And that's why it's so very important to know plenty of them. When your vocabulary is stronger, you feel more comfortable speaking with people. You can communicate your thoughts and feelings better. And you're much more likely to get what you want in life.

But this benefit will not come about from learning words that you'll never speak or seldom read. (Our speaking vocabulary is much smaller than our reading vocabulary.) So be practical. Use your time effectively, and don't look up too much. Instead, listen to those around you—especially those you admire. Take note of the words they use that you don't know. *Those* are the ones to look up first. For one thing, you'll be able to understand people better. And for another thing, you'll be able to use those words yourself.

If you have time, you can certainly look up words from newspapers and books, too, but don't mix the two. That is, don't take words from reading material and put them directly into your speaking vocabularly unless it enhances communication (instead of decorating it). They may be "reading" words, not "speaking" ones. There's a big difference. Like children, some words should be "seen, but not heard."

Vocabulary
Specific

Let's say you're reading a nonfiction book about a particular subject. It could be about anything from beetles to baseball. When you come upon a word you don't know but wish you did, which of the following comments best expresses your behavior?

1. "I have a second bookmark conveniently placed in the tome's glossary, and I turn to it promptly. But of course!"
2. "I look around a little on the page and see if I can make out the meaning somewhere else."
3. "I ignore the blasted thing. And if it happens too often, I toss the book aside, and I usually don't pick it up again, unless I'm looking for something specific."

If you answered number 1, go back and reread the previous page. You should never use "reading" words (like "tome") when you're speaking; it's obnoxious and doesn't mean you're one whit smarter. If you answered number 2, you're normal, which means you knew that looking around isn't going to help all that much. And if you answered number 3, you're also normal. All you really need to do is learn how to better evaluate books before you buy them. This is a very common problem, but it's rarely discussed.

Here are some exercises: These are groups of the same words you saw in the first half of the chapter, but now they're in their "economic" forms. (Start a new timing record for this part now; you'll compare it to the first half later.)

SUPPLY: The amount of a product that people want to sell at any particular price.

DEMAND: The amount of a product that people want to buy at any particular price.

PRODUCTION: The manufacture of goods.

CONSUMPTION: The actual use of goods.

And here are a few statements. Fill in the blanks:

1. Reports from big tomato analysts indicated that the world's _____ of salsa sauce was at an all-time low, causing prices to skyrocket.
2. Due to increased _____ from the growing number of environmental-minded customers, the manufacture of onion detectors has tripled this year.
3. In an effort to stave off unexpected foreign competition in the office-supply market, American manufacturers will introduce the _____ of electric paper clips.
4. The _____ of Japanese automobiles was at an all-time high until the much-ballyhooed style change to the shape of fish, the fins mowing down parking meters all across the country.

PRODUCTIVITY: A measure of the relationship between the cost of making a product and the value of the finished product.

COMMODITY: Any good or service available for sale.

PROFIT: The revenues received from the sale of a commodity less the cost of producing or providing it.

5. The Sooshee Corporation's _____ was twice that of the Sasheemee Corporation, whose remote-controlled spaghetti strainer was carefully designed and made from scratch.
6. Nevertheless, both companies agreed that the steam-powered cheese grater would soon become an even more valuable _____.
7. In the meantime, Sooshee is realizing a greater _____ than Sasheemee, due to the fact that Sooshee's spaghetti strainer was made from the window screens of the executive offices.

UNEMPLOYMENT: A measure of people looking for work.

UNION: An organization of workers who are wage-earners.

LABOR: The people who work for wages, as opposed to those who work for salaries or those who work for profits.

STRIKE: A halting of work by employees in order to support demands made upon their employers.

8. Last year, the _____ level was at an all-time high; even worker bees were out of jobs.

9. The _____ of airline luggage-handlers defended their right to destroy any suitcases displaying silly travel stickers.

10. At both the Sooshee and Sasheemee factories, there was the usual _____ versus management squabble over the rights of the workers to act like pelicans on their lunch hour.

11. Accordingly, workers in both factories felt they had no choice but to go on _____, carrying picket signs in their enormous beaks.

INFLATION: An increase in the average level of a l prices.

RECESSION: A period of moderate and temporary decline in economic activity.

DEPRESSION: A period of severe economic decline, marked by lower prices, falling employment, and decreased business activi-y.

12. A spokesman for the balloon industry stated yesterday that despite the current _____ rate, business was expanding.

13. It was the _____ that made executives at Sooshee and Sasheemee realize just how valuable their jobs are.

14. It was the _____ that made executives at Sooshee and Sasheemee realize just how valuable their jobs were.

Here are the answers: (1) supply, (2) demand, (3) production, (4) consumption, (5) productivity, (6) commodity, (7) profit, (8) unemployment, (9) union, (10) labor, (11) strike, (12) inflation, (13) recession, and (14) depression.

If you got fourteen to ten answers right, you clearly have these terms aced. Ten to eight right is still good. Under eight right, though, might mean you didn't take this quiz as seriously as you could have. (And we just can't imagine why you didn't.)

(Stop timing here for now.)

Specific Vocabulary

Here's a suggestion to help you increase your vocabulary in your areas of interest. Evaluate that aspect of each book before you buy it. This is seldom mentioned, but it can be of significant help, which is why we're emphasizing it.

If you'd like to learn more about a subject and aren't sure which book to choose, pick the one with a glossary first. Then, before you begin the book, read through the glossary. The point here is not to memorize it, but simply to get a brief overview and to make a mental note of the words that are contained in it. Without even trying, you'll notice these words when you come across them again in the book itself. When you're ready to begin reading, put a second bookmark in the glossary and look up the words you don't know while you read. It's beautifully simple, and it makes life easier for anyone who'd like to learn more about a subject. (Are you listening, writers and book publishers everywhere?)

But let's consider how to learn words as you read them more routinely each day. Looking up words while reading the newspaper would drive anyone crazy, so don't even think about it. Instead, try making a little list of words that trouble you, but don't add more than one word a day to the list. (That's doing too much, too soon.) When you have accumulated a dozen or so words, look them all up in the dictionary.

Better yet, buy a few small dictionaries in addition to your main one. (Don't, however, buy an "encyclopaedia of dictionaries." They're unwieldy and not usually good quality.) Some good specialized dictionaries to have around the house are a medical dictionary, a law dictionary, and several science dictionaries, according to the areas of your interest or concern. Or buy a baseball dictionary, if that's what you would like. The separate dictionaries are usually far better (having more depth) for more specific terms than your "big" dictionary, and they're usually more "accessible," too. That is, they often explain things more thoroughly rather than just stating the essential definition.

Regardless, dictionaries will help you save time. Here's an example: You're glancing through an article that relates to a remarkable breakthrough in chemistry, when you come upon the phrase, "so he added five moles . . ." You're not a chemist, so you don't know what to think. Looking up "moles" in the dictionary gives you this:

1. A growth on the skin, usually dark and sometimes hairy.
2. A small, burrowing mammal with a tough muzzle.
3. A stone wall used as a breakwater.
   And way down at the end of two paragraphs of description of things like "forefeet," you find the following:
4. The amount of a substance that has a weight in grams numerically equal to the molecular weight of the substance.

Now, if you were a chemist, you would have known that "mole" comes from the word "molecule." But you're not a chemist (which is why you should have a dictionary of chemistry handy).

Here are more exercises: (Start the timer for the last time this chapter.)

LONG RUN: A period of time that encompasses economic change.
SHORT RUN: A period of time too short to change.
MACROECONOMICS: The study of nationwide or worldwide economic conditions.
MICROECONOMICS: The study of local or narrow conditions, such as a particular area of a specific resource.
FREE-MARKET ECONOMY: A system in which any individual or business can freely participate in buying or selling goods.
PLANNED ECONOMY: A system in which the government determines the structure of the marketplace, from commodities to prices.

1. In the _____ _____, the price of glow-in-the-dark dentures is bound to come down.
2. In the _____ _____, the market for garlic-scented lip balm isn't rosy; but who knows what could happen over time?
3. After studying the _____ of the situation, an American firm quickly realized the enormous profit potential of selling ovens to the Japanese that make cooked fish raw.
4. And after studying the _____ of the situation, they realized that after enough product development, they could even dip into the home-aquarium market.
5. In a _____ economy, your neighborhood grocery store would carry a selection of two-dozen different types of sponges, some even shaped like oranges or palm trees.
6. In a _____ economy, the same store would carry only one type of sponge—and it would be brown.

GROSS NATIONAL PRODUCT (GNP): The total market value of the goods and services produced by a nation's economy in a year.

GROSS DOMESTIC PRODUCT (GDP): The market value produced by a nation's economy, excluding foreign trade and investment.

CONSUMER PRICE INDEX: A measure of living costs based on changes in the retail price of a typical "market basket."

COST OF LIVING: A measure of living costs based on calculating the price of maintaining a particular lifestyle.

7. The _____ of the primitive island nation of Upper Ugnalia was an effective folk remedy for psoriasis and four hundred pretty rocks.

8. The _____ of Upper Ugnalia was a remedy for psoriasis, after they sold the United States the four hundred pretty rocks.

9. The _____ _____ _____ indicates that middle-class Americans now earn enough to maintain a household equal to or better than that of their counterparts who tamed the West.

10. As their _____ _____ _____ increased, upper-class Americans found it difficult to afford the things they've always enjoyed: fine wine, good clothing, and decent attorneys.

And the answers? (1) long run, (2) short run, (3) macroeconomics, (4) microeconomics, (5) free-market, (6) planned, (7) GNP, (8) GDP, (9) consumer price index, and (10) cost of living. How did you do?

(You can stop timing now.)

"A powerful agent is the right word. Whenever we come upon one of those intensely right words in a book or a newspaper, the resulting effect is physical as well as spiritual, and electrically prompt."

In his "Essay on William Dean Howells," Mark Twain, as usual, knew plenty of the right words. But when reading Mark Twain or anyone else, you can't enjoy what you don't understand. Think of what it's like to be around Grandpa when he doesn't wear his hearing aid. Even though he's just "a little" deaf, he seems utterly out of the conversation. Missing just a few words removes him from the scene of the mental action. And that's what it's like for *you* when you read without a good vocabulary. You don't know what's going on. And even worse, like Grandpa, you won't know that you don't know what's going on.

But words won't cure all our intellectual ills, so before we worry over this excessively, let's have a look at what the eighteenth-century English writer Oliver Goldsmith wrote in "The Deserted Village."

In arguing too, the parson owned his skill,
For e'en though vanquished, he could argue still;
While words of learned length, and thundering sound
Amazed the gazing rustics ranged around;
And still they gazed, and still the wonder grew,
That one small head could carry all he knew.

BOOK FOUR

Writing

Thought Completion

Are you satisfied with the way you express yourself? Take the following true/false quiz and find out.

1. I have difficulty writing letters, so I avoid this as much as possible. I'd rather phone people or see them.
2. I can express myself fairly well on paper, but not orally. I'd rather write to people than talk to them.
3. When I speak with people, whatever I say seems to come out wrong.
4. In fact, other people frequently ask me to repeat what I've just said. It's embarrassing.
5. Later, I can always think of something great that I *should* have said, but didn't.

A "true" to number 1 may just mean that you don't *like* to write. Still, it's important to know how—and that avoiding paper isn't always ruinous. Avoiding people is, though. That's why a "true" to number 2 can be just as much of a handicap as a "true" to number 1. A "true" to number 3 shows that you're really suffering, whereas a "true" to number 4 shows you're at least trying. Keep it up. And a "true" to number 5 means you're just like *me!*

Here are some exercises, all related to the subject of philosophy. But don't worry. They're just exercises. You won't be getting a quiz on the subject matter. At first, just read.

The following Greeks were the most influential and (arguably) the most important philosophers who ever lived:

SOCRATES was the first of the ancient philosophers to turn his attention from the study of nature and the universe to the study of man and human behavior. He left no writings himself, but his ideas were conveyed to us by his star pupil—Plato.

PLATO employed the form of the "dialogue" to convey his (and Socrates') ideas. This was a sort of play, with characters, sets, and props. The early dialogues present Socrates in conversations that illustrate his major ideas, and the middle and later dialogues contain Plato's own treatises.

ARISTOTLE was taught by Plato. His most famous works, also dialogues, have been lost, but his treatises remain. A third group, of memoranda, has been lost, too.

Here are some questions. Without looking back at the above—this isn't a quiz about philosophy; it's an exercise in expressing yourself on paper— fill in the word (or words) that make the sentence make sense.

1. Socrates _____ the first of the ancient philosophers _____ his attention from the study of nature and the universe to the study of man and human behavior.
2. Plato _____ the form of the "dialogue" _____ _____ his (and Socrates') ideas.
3. Aristotle _____ _____ by Plato. His most famous works, also dialogues, _____ _____ lost, but his treatises ___.

Here are the central beliefs of each of these three thinkers:

SOCRATES, whose main interest was ethics, taught that virtue is knowledge and that wickedness is the result of ignorance. He felt that no one ever indulged in vice or evil acts knowingly.

PLATO, whose main interest was truth, wrote the doctrine of ideas, but not the ideas of common usage. Instead, they are something outside the mind, and he postulated a realm of truth in which ideas reside, separate from the realm of opinion.

ARISTOTLE, whose main interest was in science, insisted on the need for logic and rigor in observation. He contended that all human knowledge originates in the particular experiences of the senses, and that these form the basis of how we then perceive the universal.

Here are some more questions:

4. Socrates, whose main interest _____ ethics, _____ that virtue _____ knowledge and that wickedness _____ the result of ignorance.
5. Plato, whose main interest _____ truth, _____ the doctrine of ideas, but not the ideas of common usage.
6. Aristotle, whose main interest _____ in science, _____ on logic and rigor in observation.

Here are the answers: (1) was, to turn, (2) employed, to convey, (3) was taught, have been, remain, (4) was, taught, is, is, (5) was, wrote, and (6) was, insisted. (Synonyms or different verb tenses are fine.)

Thought Completion

Let's first consider the skill of writing. It's important not just for academic purposes, but for everyday life, as well. Suppose you have a problem with an insurance company. (And let's face it, who hasn't?) You want to straighten it out, and phone calls have been useless. "We can't do anything unless it's in writing," they tell you. And you certainly can't convey invoices and receipts orally. If you can't express yourself effectively on paper, what will you do?

Here's a suggestion to improve your writing ability. Start composing letters to the editor of your local newspapers. (Surely there are plenty of things going on in the world that you don't like.) And here's how to start. Think about the issue you've chosen and write down the most important nouns involved. (Say, "pollution," "lake," "factory," and "wildlife.") Then list some adjectives that describe your feelings about it. (Say, "unwarranted," "important," and "vanishing.") And then list the most colorful verbs that can be applied to the situation. (Say, "dumped" and "poisoned.") Then, using those words as building blocks, put together a brief letter. But put it aside; don't mail it.

Do this weekly, varying the subject, and making longer lists of words—until the day when you turn up with a letter that's really well-written and convincing. Mail that one to the editor. But don't stop there. Regardless of whether your letter is published, keep practicing and occasionally sending them your best results. Your writing will surely improve. (And you may actually make a difference.)

Here's a suggestion that will break the ice about writing personal letters—which can be good practice for writing business letters: Try a "stream-of-consciousness" technique. That is, sit down and write out your thoughts and feelings without forethought. Do it with correct grammar, however, so you learn how to organize your writing as you go along. Here's a sample letter, which I'm going to type out right now without planning and without editing:

Dear Reader:

The sun isn't shining today, and I like that, in a way. Misty days are easy on the eyes. I live hundreds of feet in the air, in a tower overlooking the river on one side and Central Park on another, and when the sun isn't shining, dusk is always something special especially as the street lights first come on.

And I wouldn't mind a fog this evening, either. You see, I'm going to be at my favorite little neighborhood restaurant around midnight, and I love walking back home in a fog, past all the old brownstones, especially if one of the horse-drawn cabs goes clopping by. It's been a long time since I've ridden in one, but it's just nice to know they're there. It's like the moon, you know. Maybe there's not much use for it, but it's nice to look up and see it still there.

I'll write again soon.

Marilyn

If your writing skills are good, but your oral skills aren't, take heart. Your writing ability proves that you have the capacity to express your thoughts in words; you probably just need more self-confidence. (Don't we all?)

Well, self-confidence grows with success, so let's try a couple of things to start giving you a sense of accomplishment. Using your writing skills, practice with telephone conversations. The next time you have to make a significant phone call, first make note of all the key words you want to use and keep the note in front of you when you call. But don't check the words off or try to work them all into the conversation or pay too much attention to them, period; if you do, you'll sound stiff or distracted. Just let the list lie there in front of you like a security blanket.

Now what about all those social events where you're sure that whatever you say will come out wrong or that you won't be able to think of the right word? It's amazing how we can totally forget the name of the author of a nice novel we read only last month when confronted with an attractive member of the opposite sex. (Don't worry; some people even forget their husbands and wives.) Well, the stream-of-consciousness technique works here, too, and you might consider trying it. For the moment, just think of yourself as a verbal impressionist and go back in time to an exciting event or a quaint little village or even your worst-ever subway ride. Talk about light and color and sound, and it'll be hard to go wrong.

Now it's time for more exercises. Remember, you don't need to worry about using the exact word. A reasonable substitute is fine.

The following statements summarize how the three ancient Greek thinkers each conceived of virtue:

SOCRATES felt that virtue meant the fulfillment of one's function as a human being, and as man is a rational being, his function is to behave rationally.

PLATO believed that virtue is linked with behavior that produces harmony and is achievable only if all aspects of the soul are fulfilling their individual functions. That is, he believed that virtue is not a matter of opinion, but is innate.

ARISTOTLE's idea of virtue consisted of a "golden mean," that is, a deliberate, careful moderation between the two extremes of "excess" (as in recklessness) and "defect" (as in cowardliness).

Here are a few questions. Fill in the blanks:

1. Socrates _____ that virtue _____ the fulfillment of one's function, as a human being, and as man _____ a rational being, his function _____ to behave rationally.
2. Plato _____ that virtue _____ _____ with behavior that _____ harmony, achievable only if all aspects of the soul _____ their individual functions.

3. Aristotle's idea of virtue _____ of a "golden mean," that is, a deliberate, careful moderation between the two extremes of 'excess" (as in recklessness) and "defect" (as in cowardliness).

Aristotle, in particular, had strong views on government. He believed that government became perverted when its rulers acted out of self-interest. He conceived of three basic types of government, each having a true form and a perverted form. The types differ according to whether there's just one ruler, a few, or many.

These are Aristotle's three basic types of government in their "true" forms:

MONARCHY: Rule by one virtuous man who governs with a view to the common interest.

ARISTOCRACY: Rule by a relatively small group of men whose degree of excellence and achievement makes them responsible and capable of command.

POLITY: Rule by a great many men that allows the abler members of the state to share in the governing of the others.

Here are those same three types of government in their "perverted" forms, which, according to Aristotle, occur when rulers turn to acting in their own self-interest instead of the common good:

TYRANNY: The rule of one man who governs for his own benefit.

OLIGARCHY: The rule of a few men who believe that because they are superior in one way, they are superior in all ways.

DEMOCRACY: The rule of a great many men who believe that because they are equal in one way, they are equal in all ways.

Also, it should be noted here that Aristotle himself believed that aristocracy was the best form of government for numerous reasons.

Here are a few questions about the basic types of government in their "true" forms:

4. MONARCHY: Rule by one virtuous man who _____ with a view to the common interest.
5. ARISTOCRACY: Rule by a relatively small group of men whose degree of excellence and achievement _____ them responsible and capable of command.

6. **POLITY: Rule by a great many men that _____ the abler members of the state to share in the governing of the others.**

And here are some questions about basic types of government in their "perverted" forms:

7. **TYRANNY: The rule of one man who _____ for his own benefit.**
8. **OLIGARCHY: The rule of a few men who _____ that because they _____ superior in one way, they _____ superior in all ways.**
9. **DEMOCRACY: The rule of a great many men who _____ that because they _____ equal in one way, they _____ equal in all ways.**

And here are the answers: (1) felt, meant, is, is, (2) believed, is linked, produces, fulfilling, (3) consisted, (4) governs, (5) make, (6) allows, (7) governs, (8) believe, are, are, and (9) believe, are, are.

How did you do? These were not quizzes on philosophy, and the sentences were left nearly intact, with almost all the important "philosophical" information right there in the question—yet they were surprisingly difficult, weren't they? Still, you probably could figure out most of them with some effort. That means you got a real workout.

───────────────────────────

Writing teaches you how to think better, and thinking better is what we're really here for, after all. Doing something "hands-on" is a great way to learn anything. Imagine what it would be like to learn how to operate a computer by watching someone else do it for a week. You would get very little out of it. Even if you already knew how to type just fine, when you finally sat down at that computer keyboard, you'd still feel lost. How different it would be if you *yourself* were sitting at the computer keyboard for a week.

And yes, this is why schoolteachers so often gave us essays to write. They know what they're doing, and writing is one of the best ways to learn to think. It drives a lot of young people nuts, and too many of them go out of their way in college to avoid courses that require papers. That's too bad, because the effort involved in writing can give those students command of a subject. It's even worse if the subject is one that is relevant to their field of interest, because they're going to be in competition with the people who *have* acquired a better grasp of it.

So take any opportunity to put your thoughts into writing. It's great exercise. And wouldn't this be a perfect time to begin writing letters to loved ones and liked ones all over the world? (It's often safer to write to "liked" ones, though. Loved ones sometimes have a habit of hanging onto your letters, and who knows? Maybe you'll be a famous writer someday and regret every letter you've ever written.)

Writing

Thought Building

How adept are you at expressing your own opinion?

1. I can write what I think and say it, too, but I never seem to be able to get my point across.
2. People always disagree with me.
3. And if I'm speaking, they even cut me off.
4. I have a very difficult time countering an argument, but I at least think of just the right thing to say *afterward!*
5. Whenever I speak, people listen. First they nod in agreement, and then they cheer. Other people find lint on their jackets; I find rose petals.

A "true" to number 1 is a common problem; you need exercise. But if number 2 is true, it probably has more to do with the company you keep and whether you're following mainstream thinking. A "true" to number 3 may mean you're a little long-winded, but if it isn't happening all the time, just mark down those interrupters as rude. As to number 4, thinking of the right thing to say afterward doesn't let you off the hook. Remember, your opponent can probably say the same thing. And if you answered "true" to number 5, either you should run for public office, or you have a teensy little "truth" problem.

Here are some exercises. And as the last section was a real workout, we're going to repeat the same subject matter, but make the exercises even tougher. Even if you think you don't know how to answer a question, try. That's a good part of the exercise right there.

The following are how the three great ancient Greek thinkers each conceived of virtue:

SOCRATES felt that virtue meant the fulfillment of one's function as a human being, and as man is a rational being, his function is to behave rationally.

PLATO believed that virtue is linked with behavior that produces harmony and is achievable only if all aspects of the soul are fulfilling their individual functions. That is, he believed that virtue is not a matter of opinion, but is innate.

ARISTOTLE's idea of virtue consisted of a "golden mean," that is, a deliberate, careful moderation between the two extremes of "excess" (as in recklessness) and "defect" (as in cowardliness).

Here are the questions. Using the words listed (in the order given), write a sentence or two that describes the philosopher named:

1. SOCRATES: virtue, fulfillment, function.
2. PLATO: virtue, behavior, harmony.
3. ARISTOTLE: virtue, moderation, extremes.

Don't stop now, though. They get easier!

Aristotle had strong views on government. These are his formulations of the three basic types of government in their "true" forms:

MONARCHY: Rule by one virtuous man who governs with a view to the common interest.

ARISTOCRACY: Rule by a relatively small group of men whose degree of excellence and achievement make them responsible and capable of command.

POLITY: Rule by a great many men that allows the abler members of the state to share in the governing of the others.

And these are the "perverted" forms of these same three types:

TYRANNY: The rule of one man who governs for his own benefit.

OLIGARCHY: The rule of a few men who believe that because they are superior in one way, they are superior in all ways.

DEMOCRACY: The rule of a great many men who believe that because they are equal in one way, they are equal in all ways.

Here are more questions: Again, using the words listed in the order given, write a sentence or two about each "form."

"True" forms:

4. **MONARCHY: one, virtuous, common interest.**
5. **ARISTOCRACY: small, excellence, capable.**
6. **POLITY: many, abler, share, others.**

"Perverted" forms:

7. **TYRANNY: one, own, benefit.**
8. **OLIGARCHY: few, superior, all.**
9. **DEMOCRACY: many, equal, all.**

There really are no right or wrong answers here. The goal was to exercise your ability to construct thoughts.

Thought Building

Remember how we discussed writing letters in the first half of this chapter? You might try getting a foreign pen pal for some "easy writing." Just think! You won't have the pressure of trying to tell your relatives what they want to hear while you will be able to tell the truth about what your life is really like. (Then again, writing to your relatives might be *great* practice!) Pen pals aren't just for kids, you know. Wouldn't it be fascinating to exchange correspondence with someone in Europe or Asia, for example, who might tell you what it's like to live in the former Soviet Union these days?

Another enjoyable and useful practice is to keep a personal journal. (I do this myself, and I bet I'll live to regret it someday.) Keep a pad of paper at your desk just for this purpose, and write down just a key word or two each time a memorable event happens or anything else you think is relevant. Then, whenever you're in the mood, sit down and construct a paragraph about each phrase you noted. That's all.

Another helpful thing to do is learn to organize your thoughts—which is not always as easy as it sounds. (For some of us, it's like taking command of a jarful of moths and getting them all to march along in single file, grouped together by family and species. And regardless of whether it's done right, they're all dead in the morning, anyway.)

One of the most common errors that occur when we express an opinion is leaving a significant part of the argument in our heads. Persuading people requires that we be able to talk about all parts of the issue—not just the most colorful ones or the most topical ones or even the ones we feel most passionate about.

A great way to practice arguing comprehensively is to arrive at the next gathering on your schedule (even a cocktail party) already armed with a topic. First, choose a significant front-page news story that interests you and read it thoroughly. As you read, note the key words on a piece of paper as you come to them. These can be either words that are relevant to the story or just words that are likely to jog your memory. Then put that list in your pocket, where it can reside like a security handkerchief throughout the evening.

Not only is it a nice technique for exercising your ability to express yourself, it also can help you get through a social event relatively undamaged, and it might even help you find a date. (But do everyone else a favor, okay? If this technique turns out to be wildly successful for you, and you find yourself turning into an orator, don't ask anyone any questions.)

And have you heard of the party game called Dictionary? Here's how it works. First, have one person select a word from the dictionary that he or she thinks no one else knows. Let's say you're the chooser. When you've chosen a word (check with everyone to make sure no one knows it), write down its definition on a piece of paper. Each other person makes up (and writes down) a definition that they hope will fool the rest, and you gather them up.

Next, you read all the definitions aloud to the group, and everyone writes down whichever one they think is the *real* definition. Anyone who guesses the correct definition gets a point, and anyone who fools other people with a wrong definition gets a point for each person he or she fooled. You continue this way until everyone has had a turn choosing a word. The highest score wins, of course.

It's crazy, I know, but it's good exercise for writing skills and creativity, and it doesn't involve doing anything immoral or illegal. (I hope that doesn't cause you to lose interest. It can be hilarious, too.)

One last idea. If it turns out that you have a touch of the sadistic in your personality, you can always hone your writing skills by sending postcards when you're on vacation to people you don't really like. I've always regarded sending a beautiful card from an exotic location as an aggressive act anyway, and if you're tired of the same old routine of writing to your friends "back home," why not consider sending those marvelous cards to people you can't stand, instead.

This can go something like, "Hi, Mortimer! Weather here on the Big Island is perfect, as usual. And the women! You wouldn't believe it, Mort! It's just like James Michener's *Hawaii*, only with hot tubs. They think guys from the mainland are the sexiest things alive, and I'm running out of money."

(We didn't say you have to be honest.)

Here are some exercises with new material on terms that relate to both ancient and modern philosophy.

These are five areas of classical philosophical investigation:

LOGIC: The study of the principles of reasoning, especially regarding structure distinguished from content.

ETHICS: The study of morals, especially regarding the choices made by an individual in relation to other individuals.

AESTHETICS: The study of taste, especially regarding the nature of beauty.

EPISTEMOLOGY: The study of the nature and origin of human knowledge.

METAPHYSICS: The study of underlying principles, especially regarding how they determine our ultimate understanding of the real world.

And here are some questions. As before, using the words listed (in order), write a sentence or two that provides a definition. Don't worry too much about accuracy. Just try.

1. LOGIC: study, reasoning, structure, content.
2. ETHICS: study, morals, choices, individual, individuals.
3. AESTHETICS: study, taste, nature, beauty.
4. EPISTEMOLOGY: study, origin, human, knowledge.
5. METAPHYSICS: study, underlying, principles, ultimate.

The following terms are two sets of paired concepts that are important to philosophical understanding:

DEDUCTION: A process of reasoning in which the given general principles lead logically to certain specific conclusions.

INDUCTION: A process of reasoning in which analysis of a specific event leads to the formulation of general principles.

A PRIORI: Knowledge that is based on general principles applied to specific instances.

A POSTERIORI: Knowledge that is based on specific instances that imply general principles.

And here are some questions: (And more sentences to write.)

6. **DEDUCTION:** reasoning, general, specific.
7. **INDUCTION:** reasoning, specific, general.
8. *A PRIORI:* knowledge, general, specific.
9. *A POSTERIORI:* knowledge, specific, general.

Here's a final (famous) allegory for extra credit. It's called "Plato's Cave." Plato, using Socrates as his mouthpiece, uses the allegory to explain the nature of human knowledge: Envision a people who've been forced to live their entire lives imprisoned in a cave, unable to even turn around. A fire is blazing away behind them, but all they can see are their own shadows on the wall in front of them. If they've never seen anything else, they believe these shadows are reality. Likewise, we all mistakenly think the world as we perceive it is the real world, even though we actually are seeing only the "shadows" of reality. So here's your final question—once again explain the term using the words in the order given.

10. **PLATO'S CAVE:** people, imprisoned, cave, fire, shadows, reality, likewise, mistakenly, perceive, world, "shadows."

I'm sure you noticed how, throughout this chapter, whenever you were asked to use words to build a thought, you were given the key words of the thought in a logical order. Because much of the material was not wholly familiar to you, we chose to use the order of the original sentence, explaining the idea to keep things clear.

But there are other logical kinds of order, of course, and all of them will work well when you need to build a presentation. You can order your words chronologically, or from most important to least important, or from general to specific. Aside from the fact that a logical organization is far more readily understandable to your listener or reader, it makes it a lot easier for *you* to put together your presentation.

This goes for everything from writing a paragraph to send the insurance company to preparing your doctoral dissertation on Jean-Paul Sartre's examination of the individual as a responsible but dreadfully lonely little being adrift in a vast, meaningless universal sea and burdened with a terrifying freedom of choice. (An existentialist is not someone you want to invite to your next St. Patrick's Day party, although they're not really so bad on Halloween.)

Organization makes life easier, and writing is no exception. Write down your key points as you think of them, arrange them logically, and half the work is done.

Part Two

COMPREHENSION

BOOK FIVE

General Comprehension

Understanding How

How's your general comprehension of how things work? Here's another true/false quiz.

1. I am overwhelmed by science: I can't even understand why my toaster does what it does, much less my furnace.
2. I'm not too bad around the house, but I didn't even known there *was* an ozone layer before I heard there was a hole in it.
3. I have to get out all the instruction booklets every time I need to change my digital clocks every spring and fall.
4. I know a little bit about science, but I can't seem to learn how to operate all of the options on my VCR.
5. I'm capable of making decisions on such things as global warming and the Strategic Defense Initiative.

A "true" to number 1 probably indicates that you're missing a few basic science courses. Relax. Most people are. A "true" to number 2 is perfectly normal. So is a "true" to number 3 and number 4, but it's irritating, isn't it? We'll show you how to overcome that later in this chapter. A "true" to number 5, however, is far more common than it should be. Even people who can't explain their carburetors have opinions on these weighty scientific matters!

As Agatha Christie's famous fictional detective Hercule Poirot said, "Let us exercise our little gray cells!" The exercises to help you expand your ability to comprehend information will be taken from the subject of human anatomy. Nervous? Well, now you can find out why.

The following passage describes the basic elements and functions of the nervous system:

The nervous system controls all functions of the body. The brain and the spinal cord form the "central nervous system," and the somatic and autonomic system form the "peripheral nervous system." Messages travel from one nerve cell to another using electricity and chemicals. The electrical signals are converted into chemical signals at the point where a sending cell meets a receiving cell. But they don't touch. Instead, they communicate across a gap called a synapse, using molecules to do so.

Here are a few questions:

1. HOW are electrical signals used by the nervous system?
2. HOW are chemical signals used by the nervous system?
3. HOW do messages get across the synaptical gap?

Here's a short passage about the unsung hero of the human body, the endocrine system:

The endocrine is the "other" of the body's two major control systems, although most people have barely heard of it. Together with the nervous system, with which it interacts, these systems coordinate most bodily functions.

The endocrine system uses hormones to help the body provide a constant chemical environment (such as sugar in the blood), produce long-term changes (such as growth), and short-term ones (such as fighting infection). Perhaps even more surprising, it has a powerful effect on emotions, hunger, thirst, and (no surprise here) sex drives.

And here are a few questions:

4. HOW does the endocrine system control blood sugar, growth, and infection-fighting?
5. HOW does the endocrine system control emotions?
6. HOW does it control hunger, thirst, and sex drives?

The following describes the basic elements and functions of the circulatory system:

Like an elaborate subway system, the network of arteries, veins, and capillaries uses blood to supply nutrients and oxygen to the body and to retrieve carbon dioxide, water, and waste. All of this activity is powered by the heart, which expands and contracts to either force blood away from it or pull blood into it. This "beating" is produced by a center (in the upper-right chamber) that acts as a natural electrical pacemaker.

And a few more questions:

7. HOW are nutrients and gases transported through the body?
8. HOW is the blood flow controlled?
9. HOW is the heartbeat controlled?

If you're unsure of any answer, reread that passage again.

Understanding How

Here's an important suggestion: When you're reading (or listening) for comprehension, try to keep your goal in mind. Remember those aspects of a story that newspaper reporters are supposed to include? They're "who," "what," "where," "why," and "when." The one they usually leave out is "how"—but that's the one that's most important to comprehension. Notice that you'll often find that question answered in the science section of a newspaper, while science stories reported on the front page will seldom include "how." That's because the newspaper is more interested in reporting than it is in teaching, but you don't have to be hindered by that.

When you're paying attention, think "how." And as that's our focus in this half of the chapter, try it for yourself in the coming pages. Keep the word (or concept) "how" uppermost in your mind when you read the passages to come. Also, try to transfer this technique to other areas in your daily life.

And here's another suggestion—the one we promised you when we asked about digital clocks and videocassette recorders. Apart from comprehending words, you want to know how to comprehend "things," too, and here's an active, fun way to achieve that goal: *Don't* read the instruction booklet first (unless there's a possible hazard, of course). Instead, examine the object and try to figure out how to operate it yourself. And don't give up unless there's a pressing need. (Like your favorite show is coming on in five minutes. That's important!)

This won't be easy at first, but if you continue to do it, time after time, consulting an instruction booklet only when progress is (or seems) impossible, you'll gain a familiarity with household appliances, mechanical devices, and electronic gadgetry that will transfer all across your life and lifestyle.

A few years ago, I tried this with digital clocks. Finding myself with the bothersome task of changing a couple of dozen of them every spring and fall, ranging from my wristwatch to my computer to the microwave at home, I first had to round up all the little instruction booklets. And looking up the relevant sections in each one was actually more annoying than the changing of the time itself. So I dispensed with the instructions and simply pushed buttons, fairly randomly at first. But with attention and experience, patterns began to emerge. I began to get a "feel" of how these things operate, and it became so easy that I haven't touched those irksome little booklets for years now.

It even works this way with cooking. As long as you only follow recipes, you'll never be able to whip up something from scratch on your own or be creative on a rainy winter night with whatever you find in the cupboard. People who have cooked good meals with recipes for *years* can find themselves at a total loss when putting together something as simple as a nice pizza. You can use the most expensive "extra extra virgin" olive oil, and the freshest mozzarella and Parmesan, but it still won't taste like a pizza without that touch of oregano and/or basil.

It's time for more exercises. Take a deep breath.

The following describes the basic elements and functions of (you guessed it) the respiratory system:

Air is inhaled and then passes through a thin tube called the trachea before entering the lungs. There, after branching into a network of air sacs, oxygen and carbon dioxide are exchanged with the tiny capillaries that will ultimately carry the oxygen to the rest of the body while the carbon dioxide is being exhaled. A respiratory center in the brain determines the pace of breathing, drawing the muscle sheet beneath the lungs (called the diaphragm) downward and upward, pulling air into the body or forcing it out.

1. HOW does air get to the lungs?
2. HOW do oxygen and carbon dioxide get exchanged?
3. HOW does the diaphragm help in breathing?

Here's a brief overview of the workings of the digestive system:

The digestive system is essentially a thirty-foot-long canal. The process of digestion begins in the mouth, where ingested food is first broken down, both by chewing and enzymes. After passing through the esophagus, food is further processed in the stomach before entering the small intestine. As the broken-down food travels through this long tube, looped back and forth again and again, nearly all of the food's nutrients are absorbed into the body. Then, after everything useful is extracted, waste passes out through the large intestine.

Here are a few questions:

4. HOW does food get broken down in the mouth?
5. HOW does food get from the mouth to the stomach?
6. HOW does the small intestine play a leading role?

And last, here's a brief overview of the workings of the urinary system:

Urination is the result of two functions, one of which may come as a surprise to those of us who didn't attend medical school: the filtering of blood and the removal of excess water. The kidneys monitor the balance of blood constituents and maintain a fluid balance in the body. As a result of both these functions, urine—which contains injurious and waste products from the blood, in addition to water—is produced continuously and sent to the bladder, where it is stored until emptied.

7. HOW is the body's blood monitored?
8. HOW is the body's excess water removed?
9. HOW does urine serve a dual purpose?

Again, if you felt unsure of the answer to any particular question, you should go back and reread the relevant passage, keeping "how" in mind. And remember, this is not an anatomy quiz, but rather an exercise in comprehension.

Alert readers may notice at this point that we neglected to mention the reproductive system, often considered to be one of the highlights in human anatomy. We're not prudish, mind you, but instead decided to save the space for things you *didn't* know.

Probably the best way to learn "how" is to interact with the subject, not just to observe—as many of us learned the hard way with computers. Of course, that isn't always possible, no matter how much motivation we have. Still, we should try, to whatever extent is possible.

One of the best, most accessible texts I've seen on the subject is called *The Way Things Work* by David Macaulay. Although this is more of a visual guide to the world of machines, it is instructive not only as it relates specifically to a particular "machine," but also in its underlying approach to the whole notion of "how"—although you won't find that anywhere in the text.

What is (almost) an indispensable tool in learning "how"? Visualization. That means observing *actively*, not merely keeping your eyes open. Start paying attention to how the world works, and a whole new (and fascinating) level of understanding will open up for you. Is there a building going up nearby? Great. Go on over there and take note of what's happening (you might want to carry your binoculars with you each day). What material has just arrived? And where is it being hauled? Why is the construction elevator located on one side rather than another?

You don't need an exact answer to every question, and that's not the point, anyway. To learn "how" about anything from buildings to birds, you need to learn to develop an inquiring mind and a healthy curiosity. This will make you a happier, more knowledgeable person—not to mention a more interesting one.

General Comprehension

Understanding Why

And how's your general comprehension of *why* things work? Here's another true/false quiz.

1. When I'm given instructions, either at work at at school, I seldom ask "why."
2. Frankly, I seldom care.
3. I'd often like to know the reason for things, but I've noticed that people find such questions intrusive.
4. I do pretty well with "how" things work, but "why" just doesn't interest me much.
5. Isn't "why" just for scientists, anyway?

A "true" to number 1 may be just a reasonable concern about not intruding where you're not wanted (or where you don't belong), but a "true" to number 2 may mean you lack curiosity. Is it possible you're a little depressed? If not, you probably answered "true" to number 3. And a "true" to number 4 is normal for a mechanical mind, but a "true" to number 5 indicates that you may be ignoring a very important facet of intelligence that could bring you a great deal of pleasure and make your life easier.

Read on.

Here are more exercises, most of which will expand on the subjects we introduced in the first half of the chapter. The goal is to exercise your ability to understand "why"—and specifically, why the body does some of the things it does.

Let's return to the nervous system and consider some of the things that can go wrong with it:

Pain, which has a bad reputation, and understandably so, is beneficial in at least one way. The stimulation of the body's nerves called "pain receptors" is an indication that something is wrong and should be investigated.

Paralysis is the loss of motor function in a portion of the body, such as a leg, the entire lower torso, or more. If the damage is between the spinal cord and muscle, the affected part loses tone and withers. If the paralysis is due to a brain injury, however, a spinal cord connection is maintained, and the muscle tightens in spasm.

Stroke is the rupture of a blood vessel in the brain or a sudden blockage of the blood supply to the brain. The damage occurs when the affected brain cells are deprived of oxygen and die, causing impairment of function in the parts of the body controlled by that portion of the brain.

Here are a few questions:

1. WHY can pain be considered beneficial?
2. WHY can paralysis sometimes result in withering and sometimes not?
3. WHY does stroke cause damage?

The following are brief descriptions of common disorders of the endocrine system:

Diabetes is a disturbance of carbohydrate metabolism in which much of the sugar in the body cannot be used by the cells, accumulating in the blood, instead.

Thyroid problems can cause the body's metabolism (the rate at which nutrients are transformed into energy) to either speed up or slow down. With too much secretion of hormones, weight loss and serious emotional disturbance can occur; with too little secretion, the result can be mental and physical retardation in children.

4. WHY does diabetes cause a higher blood sugar level?
5. WHY do thyroid problems cause a change of metabolism?

And here are some problems that can affect the circulatory system:

When you're wounded, the kamikaze platelets in your blood race to the rescue, dying in the process. They stick to the edges of the wound, closing it with a plug, and if the wound is serious, they seal it with a clot.

High blood pressure, unattended, can cause strokes, heart attacks, and aneurysms, in which a weak spot in an arterial wall bulges out. If a major artery in the body bursts, the rapid drop in blood pressure can cause sudden death.

Immune-system failures can be deadly. Deficiencies such as AIDS result in a loss of the white blood cells that fight infection, allowing opportunistic diseases to run rampant through the body.

6. WHY does a wound close with a plug or a clot?
7. WHY can an aneurysm cause sudden death?
8. WHY are white blood cells so important?

Understanding Why

"How" may be the most important word when it comes to comprehension, but "why" ranks a close second.

One of the best ways to comprehend a paragraph, a book, or an entire subject is to ask questions about it. The importance of doing this cannot be overestimated, partly because it works so well and partly because we all suffer from a psychological block about it, at least to some degree. Even the most knowledgeable people can be shy about asking questions, and for all sorts of reasons. There's the fear of making a pest out of yourself, of course, but far more prevalent is the fear of looking "dumb." I have it myself. People expect me to have all the answers myself, and they're always shocked when I ask questions. It's not a situation I enjoy, but it's one I have to live with.

Comprehension is an active process. You don't get it by simply leaving your ears open. Learn to ask questions, and you'll learn a way of dealing with material that puts you in the driver's seat. Let's say your car didn't start this morning, and a fellow with a tow truck is now bending over the engine with you. "Vapor lock," he says, slamming the hood back down. "Vapor lock," you repeat to yourself as you watch your car retreat down the driveway, trunk first. That's not good enough! What *is* vapor lock? Ask him. And when he tells you that it's a pocket of vaporized gasoline in the fuel line that obstructs the normal flow of fuel, don't stop there. Ask him why it occurs. And if he says he just told you, ask him again. "What" isn't "why."

Granted, the mechanic should probably be given a copy of this book, but you shouldn't give up just because someone is tired of talking to you—at least not when you're paying for their services. But the same thing applies to school and the workplace. You probably have good judgment. Use it. While you don't want to annoy an instructor or an employer by taking too much of his or her limited time or just plain interrupting too frequently, don't use that reasonable concern to cover up a fear of looking "dumb" because you're asking a question. Ask!

But you can't ask questions of a book, can you? (And you wouldn't *dream* of telephoning the author, would you?) There is, however, something you *can* do, and I do it myself when I run across something difficult. While reading, don't stop too often to puzzle over a passage or a page. Instead, read the entire book at a rapid, steady clip, and then read it again. A surprising amount of what you didn't get the first time will come clear in the re-reading. It's something like seeing a movie twice. The second time you see it, you notice all sorts of significant things that you completely missed the first time around.

How about a real textbook, you ask—the very model of the exercise of comprehension? Try this. Before you read a chapter, read the exercises for it. Not only will they cover the important points, they'll also give you an idea of the goal you should be keeping in mind as you read. Is time emphasized? Money? Political fortunes? Or personal ones? Look to the subjects the exercises review for the keys to comprehension.

It's time for more exercises. Why? you may ask. (No, no, not yet!)

The following are a few interesting facts about disorders of the digestive system:

Stomach acid is powerful enough to dissolve a razor blade, so it secretes a thick, protective mucus to keep from digesting itself. Ulcers are caused by a failure of this mechanism.

Heartburn, the familiar burning sensation behind the breastbone, has nothing to do with the heart. Instead, it is caused by stomach acid backing up into the lower esophagus.

Gallstones can be very painful, but the gallbladder can be removed entirely without ill effect. Afterward, bile flows directly from the liver to the small intestine.

And here are a few more questions:

1. WHY doesn't the stomach digest itself?
2. WHY does heartburn occur?
3. WHY can the entire gallbladder be removed?

And here are a few facts about problems with the respiratory system:

A sneeze is the body's primitive method of expelling an irritant from the nasal passages, and it is usually triggered by tiny particles that have settled on the highly sensitive membranes of the nose.

A cough is another method for expelling an irritant, except that the particles are located lower in the respiratory system. Chronic coughing, however, can be symptomatic of disease.

A "cold" is actually caused by one or more of some two hundred different viruses, which is one reason they're so difficult to treat. Not only are antibiotics ineffective against viruses, there also are too many viruses to effectively track quickly, anyway.

And a few more questions:

4. WHY do we sneeze?
5. WHY do we cough?
6. WHY are colds so difficult to treat?

And lastly, here are a couple of facts about problems of the urinary system:

Kidney stones are usually composed of calcium that has crystallized out of the urine. While most kidney stones are small enough to pass through the urinary tract and out of the body, larger ones can become lodged there. They not only cause excruciating pain, but obstruct the kidney, as well. Happily, doctors now can dissolve many of these stones by using a machine that generates shock waves, turning the calcium deposits into tiny particles that will pass out of the body more easily.

The kidneys trickle urine into the bladder twenty-four hours a day, but the bladder doesn't signal for urination until it reaches about sixteen ounces. It contracts to start urination, at the same time closing off the ureters in order to prevent urine from flowing back up to the kidneys.

7. WHY don't kidney stones require surgical removal as often as they used to?
8. WHY don't we have the urge to urinate constantly?

The keys to comprehension are "how" and "why"—although not always in that order and not necessarily in that order of importance. After all, which is more important: "how" we should build more nuclear weaponry, or "why" we should? That is, "how" is often the question of doers, and "why" is often the question of thinkers, and goodness knows we dearly need both of them in this modern world.

This brings us to an important aspect of comprehension, one that must be emphasized, especially in this age of exploding information: There is much that *cannot* be comprehended, and you shouldn't feel troubled or take it personally if you find that to be the case. Of course, a significant percentage of new information is just plain difficult, even for the best-educated and brightest among us, but that's not the part we're talking about here. No, it's the *rest* of that incomprehensible information we mean: It's the stuff that's *wrong*. Just plain *wrong*.

Ptolemy believed that the Earth was the center of our solar system. Copernicus showed that Ptolemy was wrong and believed that the planets moved in circular orbits around the sun. Kepler showed that Copernicus was wrong and believed that the planets moved in elliptical orbits around the sun. All along the way, people were "comprehending" utterly false information.

Kepler also thought that the stars were all contained within a thin shell somewhere outside the solar system. So you don't comprehend Einstein? Don't worry about it. Just wait.

BOOK SIX

Reasoning
Mathematical

Do any of these statements apply to you? That is, are any of them true?

1. I can't figure out anything unless math is used.
2. I can figure out anything unless math is used.
3. I'm not very good at figuring things out unless every step is clearly outlined.
4. And as far as I'm concerned, logic is something that only Spock enjoys using. (Hmmm. Does Spock actually *enjoy* logic?)
5. In fact, I'm still a little confused by those first two questions!

A "true" to number 1 can mean that you like tight reasoning—fine in its place, though its place isn't everywhere. But a "true" to number 2, number 3, and/or number 4 may mean that your reasoning skills are weak. And a "true" to number 5 is normal, which may mean that your reasoning skills, if not actually weak, are not as good as they could be. Those first two statements came out of left field, we know, but we also know that the size of left field varies from ball park to ball park, and this book isn't Shea Stadium! If you had to read them more than twice, you need a little exercise!

So here are a few exercises. After thinking long and hard (and reasoning this all through, of course), we came to the conclusion that the best subject to use for exercises in mathematical reasoning is . . . well, mathematics!

The following exercises show how to solve for an unknown number x, and the goal is to isolate x on one side of the equal sign by eliminating all the other numbers that appear with it. For the initial exercises, just follow along with the reasoning, even with the parts you already know. (Remember, this is an exercise in reasoning, and reading the material will be exercise in itself.) When you reach the second set, you're on your own. (But the answers will follow.)

A basic equation is, say, $x + 5 = 9$. This means that a certain number plus five equals nine, and x represents that certain number. Intuitively, we know that the way to find that number is to subtract five from nine, which is the same as subtracting five from both sides of the equation. This makes sense because both sides must remain equal. Therefore, $x = 4$.

The following problems show how x can be determined when the processes are less intuitive and more "reason"able:

1.   The equation? $2x + 3 = 11$
      We subtract three from each side, and we're left with:
$$2x = 8$$
      So we divide each side by two, and we're left with:
$$x = 4$$
To check our answer, we substitute four for x in the original equation:
$$2(4) + 3 = 11$$
So:
$$8 + 3 = 11 \text{ (Correct).}$$

2.   The equation? $3x - 7 = 8$
      We add seven to each side (so that we can cancel out the -7 on x's side of the equation), and we're left with:
$$3x = 15$$
      So we divide each side by three, and we're left with:
$$x = 5$$
To check our answer, we substitute five for x in the original equation:

$$3(5) - 7 = 8$$

So:

$$15 - 7 = 8 \text{ (Correct)}.$$

3. **The equation?** $\qquad 2(x + 4) = 28$

We remove the parentheses by multiplying each number within it by two:

$$2x + 8 = 28$$

We subtract eight from each side, and we're left with:

$$2x = 20$$

So we divide each side by two, and we're left with:

$$x = 10$$

To check our answer, we substitute ten for x in the original equation and multiply the sum of the parentheses by two:

$$2(10 + 4) = 28$$

So:

$$20 + 8 = 28 \text{ (Correct)}.$$

Remember, don't skim these numbers. This is exercise.

4. **The equation?** $\qquad 5(x - 3) = 5$

We remove the parentheses by multiplication, as above:

$$5x - 15 = 5$$

We add fifteen to each side, and we're left with:

$$5x = 20$$

So we divide each side by five, and we're left with:

$$x = 4$$

To check our answer, we substitute four for x in the original equation:

$$5(4 - 3) = 5$$

So:

$$20 - 15 = 5 \text{ (Correct.)}$$

Here are a few word problems that use the same methods illustrated above (and even the same equations). Work through them without looking back:

1. An ant making off with a club sandwich hauls it a total of 11 feet in 2 and 1/2 minutes. Sprinting at a steady pace, he lasts only 3 feet into the third minute before the sandwich's owner steps on him. How far did the ant run during each of the first two minutes?

2. A frog and a five-year-old boy eat some flies in the course of an afternoon. The boy ate 8 flies, but, all told, he had actually tried 3 times as many flies as the frog. Due to a finicky nature, however, the boy decided to spit out 7 of them. How many flies did the frog eat?

3. A crayfish, a shrimp, and a squid have found themselves caught by a fisherman, who callously tosses them onto a scale. Combined, they weigh 28 ounces. The shrimp weighs 4 ounces, and the crayfish weighs two times as much as the weight of the shrimp and squid combined. How much does the squid weigh?

4. A squirrel living in Central Park has been having trouble with his tree hole being broken into by masked raccoons, and he's down to a measly 5 mixed nuts after the latest theft of 3 acorns. But he has never been thrilled by acorns, anyway, and if he now has five times as many mixed nuts as he does acorns, how many acorns did he have in the first place?

Here are the answers: (1) 4 feet, (2) 5 flies, (3) 10 ounces, and (4) 4 acorns.

What a surprise, right? And these problems used the same equations that you dismissed just a few minutes ago as "too easy"! If you got two (or more) problems wrong or found them much harder than you expected, then you've got good evidence that your reasoning skills need the exercise they just had. In other words, you did fine with the steps that were outlined (which means you understood the reasoning perfectly well), but you had difficulty doing it on your own.

And now we can tell you a cold, hard fact that we've avoided mentioning up until now. You've been doing basic algebra! Somehow, the term "mathematics" doesn't strike nearly as much fear into people as "algebra," and we didn't want you to skip past this chapter entirely. But now that you have come this far, it doesn't seem so bad, does it? (Or does it?)

Mathematical Reasoning

Developing and strengthening our ability to reason sounds like a particularly daunting task, probably because so many people think it's something you're born with, like blond hair or blue eyes (or money). But just look at the difference in reasoning power between a normal person who has never been to school and a highly educated scientist. It's night and day, right? That's a good indication that reasoning power is learned, and you can do it if you try.

The more you use your reasoning powers, the better you'll get at it, and mathematical reasoning is certainly included. One trick you might try is drawing pictures. Sounds elementary, doesn't it? Almost embarrassing to do? Well, that's why people don't do it, and they're the losers for thinking that way. Maybe those people are just visual types, for heaven's sake. What's wrong with that? Do what works—and if drawing pictures works for you, do it! Anyway, visualization is far more natural than working with words; it suits our physical nature better.

Consider how much more difficult it is to describe something in words than it is to draw a picture of it. Just remember that old equation from years back: 1 picture = 1000 words. Then think, how useful would your television instruction booklet be if it had no illustrations? How would you like to connect your cable system to your television to your videocassette recorder to your stereo outfit with an instruction book that described it in words, but had *no illustrations?*

As an example, here's a nice, yet tricky, little problem in reasoning: If a striped bass weighs five pounds plus half its own weight, how much does it weigh? There's nothing at all wrong or misleading about that sentence, but it makes you blink and read it over a couple of times, doesn't it? (And no, it doesn't weigh seven and a half pounds. How could it both weigh five pounds and seven and a half pounds at the same time?) Try visualizing it, as with our balance scale below:

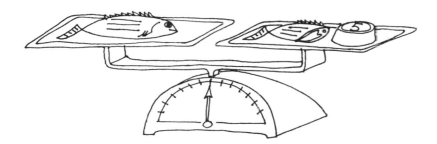

On one pan, there's a striped bass. On the other, there's a five-pound weight and half a striped bass. According to the problem, the scale balances. Looking at the right side of the above scale, then, you can see that the five-pound weight is taking the place of the front half of the fish. And that means another five-pound weight could take the place of the tail half of the fish, as below:

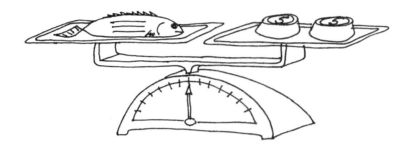

So it's now clear that the striped bass weighs ten pounds. But it wasn't so clear in words, was it? You can either draw a picture literally or envision the problem mentally, but the suggestion is the same: Visualize.

And now it's time for more exercises:

1. **The equation?** $x + 8 = 4x - 4$
    We subtract x from each side, and we're left with:
    $$8 = 3x - 4$$
    So we add 4 to each side, and we're left with:
    $$12 = 3x$$
    So we divide each side by three, and we're left with:
    $$4 = x$$
    To check our answer, we substitute four for x in the original equation:
    $$4 + 8 = 16 - 4$$
    So:
    $$12 = 12 \text{ (Correct.)}$$

2. **The equation?** $3(x + 2) = 3(8 - x)$
    To remove the parentheses by multiplication:
    $$3x + 6 = 24 - 3x$$

We add $3x$ to each side, and we're left with:

$$6x + 6 = 24$$

So we subtract six from each side, and we're left with:

$$6x = 18$$

So we divide each side by six, and we're left with:

$$x = 3$$

To check our answer, we substitute three for x in the original equation:

$$3(3 + 2) = 3(8 - 3)$$

So:

$$9 + 6 = 24 - 9$$

And so:

$$15 = 15 \text{ (Correct.)}$$

3. **The equation?**

$$\frac{x}{10} = \frac{1}{5}$$

We remove the fractions by multiplication:

$$(10)\frac{x}{10} = (10)\frac{1}{5}$$

And then by simplification:

$$\cancel{(10)}\,\frac{x}{\cancel{10}} = \overset{2}{\cancel{(10)}}\,\frac{1}{\cancel{5}}$$

And we're left with: $\qquad\qquad x = 2$

To check our answer, we substitute two for x in the original equation:

$$\frac{2}{10} = \frac{1}{5} \text{ (Correct)}.$$

4. **The equation?**

$$\frac{x - 1}{3} = \frac{x - 2}{2}$$

We remove the fractions by multiplication:

$$(6)\frac{x - 1}{3} = (6)\frac{x - 2}{2}$$

And then by simplification:

$$\overset{2}{\cancel{(6)}}\,\frac{x - 1}{\cancel{3}} = \overset{3}{\cancel{(6)}}\,\frac{x - 2}{\cancel{2}}$$

And we're left with: $\qquad 2(x - 1) = 3(x - 2)$

We remove the parentheses by multiplication:

$$2x - 2 = 3x - 6$$

So we add six to each side, and we're left with:

$$2x + 4 = 3x$$

So we subtract $2x$ from each side, and we're left with:

$$4 = x$$

To check our answer, we substitute four for x in the original equation:

$$\frac{4 - 1}{3} = \frac{4 - 2}{2}$$

So:

$$\frac{3}{3} = \frac{2}{2} \text{ (Correct.)}$$

Here are a few more word problems that use the same methods illustrated above (as well as the same equations). Again, work through them without looking back.

Wait! Don't put the book down for the day yet. Those equations are fresh in your mind, and now's the time to get through the next exercises. You're warmed up. Try them, even if you think you're going to get a couple of them wrong:

1. An aardvark has a number of termites in his deep freeze. The number of termites plus 8 aphids is equal to 4 less than 4 times the number of termites. How many termites does the aardvark have?

2. A dingo can snatch a certain number of babies. Three times the sum of the number of Australian babies plus 2 tourists' babies is equal to 3 times the sum of 8 tourists' babies minus that certain number of Australian babies. How many Australian babies can a dingo snatch?

3. A Portuguese man-of-war can sting a certain number of bathers. A tenth of the number he can sting is 1/5. So how many bathers can the man-of-war sting?

4. The tenants of the St. Louis Zoo Reptile House were all crawling and slithering around the locker room after a good workout, and as usual, they began to brag about their hunting prowess. This irritated the tortoise, because he had lately taken a liking to clumps of weeds and didn't bother to hunt much, not that he could ever catch anything interesting anyway. So after listening to them go on and on (and on) for a while, he decided to shut them up by giving them a problem using the information he had just heard.

(Also, he knew that most of them weren't too bright and were just there on athletic scholarship, anyway.)

This is what it amounted to: The number of small furry mammals the garter snake could devour less the 1 fly the gecko could gulp down, all divided by the 3 eggs the rattlesnake could eat was equal to that same number of small furry animals minus the 2 stick insects the iguana could manage, all divided by the tortoise's two clumps of weeds. How many small furry mammals could the garter snake devour?

Here are the answers: (1) 4 termites, (2) 3 Australian babies, (3) 2 bathers, and (4) 4 small furry mammals.

Okay, we'll admit it. That was ridiculous. But we'll bet you got plenty of mental exercise puzzling out those "4 plus 3 less 1 divided by 6" sentences, didn't you? And you got plenty of exercise putting it into equation form, didn't you? And that's the point of all this, isn't it? (You're supposed to say "yes.")

To exercise your mathematical reasoning ability, we used algebra for a reason. You can think of math as logic with numbers attached, and algebra represents this kind of symbolic logic at its most elemental. That doesn't mean it's easy, of course. The word "elemental" (as opposed to "elementary") connotes the "essence" of the subject, and algebra fits that definition very well. In the more abstruse areas of mathematics, we no longer deal with the real world as we know it and instead use known mathematical operations as tools to replace what can't be directly grasped. Take finding a "cube root" as an example. There's a known method, and people can do it with a pencil and paper, but they're only following rules, not manipulating the concepts themselves.

Take every chance to exercise your mathematical reasoning ability in everyday life. This is an area that becomes incredibly rusty—and fast. For example, unless you have real reason to believe it will save you money, do your own tax returns. We know it may cost you some time, but you'll get the benefit of the mental exercise, and that's every bit as important as physical exercise. After all, going to the gym takes time, too. And even if it's faster to take the elevator than to climb a few flights of stairs, it's better to climb the stairs. (But don't be afraid to use a calculator. Calculators don't take the place of reasoning; they only increase your efficiency. It doesn't help your reasoning ability to do long division by hand.) Give your mind at least as much exercise as you give your body.

Reasoning
Logical

How logical are you? Try this true/false quiz.

1. When I read, "If *a* equals *b*, and *b* equals *c*, then *a* equals *c*," I can't help but wonder why we even *have* an alphabet if all the letters are going to mean the same thing.
2. I don't *want* to be logical; the world is not logical; if the world were logical, there would be no poverty, disease, war, or attorneys.
3. There's a place for logic, and it's not a very big place.
4. I'm logical at work. Everyplace else, forget it.
5. Why, *everything* I do is based on logic, of course. What else is so accurate and reliable? I should trust my *heart* when it comes to something as important as marriage? Are you kidding?

A "true" to number 1 indicates that you don't know how to use logic at all. And a "true" to number 2 makes no sense. All the things listed (even attorneys) may be perfectly logical. Just because something is logical doesn't mean it's going to be pretty. Answers of "true" to number 3 and number 4 are perfectly normal, but a "true" to number 5 (and we know you didn't answer that) may indicate an obsessive or compulsive disorder or denial of emotion for some other reason.

Here are a few exercises. In the same way that math problems were the best way to exercise your mathematical reasoning, so logic problems are (logically) the best way to exercise your logical reasoning.

To solve these types of problems, it can be helpful to construct a chart, and we'll show you how to do that first. Suppose you met several people at a party and tried to remember each of their names. You know you met a Mr. Smith, a Mr. Jones, a Mr. Brown, and a Mr. White (this was a very average party, remember), and you know they had each been wearing one of the following, in no particular order: a red tie, a striped tie, a polka-dot tie, and a paisley tie. You call the host of the party, who gives you the following four clues:

A. White and Smith don't like red ties.
B. Jones talked to the man with a polka-dot tie all evening.
C. Smith never met Jones or the man with a paisley tie.
D. Brown and the man with a paisley tie were old friends.

Here's the grid you should make to solve the problem:

	Smith	Jones	Brown	White
Red tie				
Striped tie				
Polka-dot tie				
Paisley tie				

Now, read through the clues and enter a check for an established fact and an "x" for an impossibility.

A. White and Smith don't like red ties, so enter x's in the boxes where "White" and "red tie" intersect and where "Smith" and "red tie" intersect.

B. Jones talked to the man with a polka-dot tie all evening, so Jones wasn't wearing that tie himself. Enter an x at Jones/polka-dot.

C. Smith never met Jones or the man with the paisley tie, so neither Smith nor Jones was wearing that tie. Enter two more x's.

D. Brown and the man with a paisley tie were old friends, so Brown wasn't wearing that tie either. Enter another x.

Now the chart should look like this:

	Smith	Jones	Brown	White
Red tie	x			x
Striped tie				
Polka-dot tie		x		
Paisley tie	x	x	x	

Notice that there are three x's along the paisley tie line. We can reason that White must have been the one with the paisley tie. Put a checkmark at White/paisley and add x's to the remaining boxes in his column.

Now let's go back and reread the clues. Jones talked to the man with the polka-dot tie all evening, so if Jones and Smith never met, then Smith wasn't wearing a polka-dot tie. As soon as we put an x in Smith/polka-dot, we know that he was wearing the striped tie. And with three x's in the polka-dot tie column, we now know that Brown was wearing it. That leaves only one man and one tie. Clearly, Jones was the man wearing the red tie.

Here are a couple of problems for you to solve on your own:

1. You have three amphibians as pets: a toad, a salamander, and a newt. You keep one in the bathtub, one in the kitchen sink, and one next to your bed. Who lives where?
   A. The toad is friends with the one in the bathroom.
   B. The salamander is the same age as the one in the bedroom.
   C. The newt and the one in the bedroom haven't met.

	Toad	Salamander	Newt
Bathroom			
Kitchen			
Bedroom			

2. You have three fish as pets: a goldfish, a gourami, and a nice, shiny halibut. You don't know much about fish and wonder which is which.

Then you read in a little book that each fish has a favorite toy: a ceramic bell-diver, an aerating sea chest, or plastic algae. Who is which?

A. The goldfish is allergic to plastic algae.

B. The gourami is terrified of the ceramic bell-diver and also dislikes each of the other fish.

C. The fish that plays with the aerating sea chest has a crush on the halibut.

	Goldfish	Gourami	Halibut
Ceramic bell-diver			
Aerating sea chest			
Plastic algae			

Here are the answers: (1) The toad is in the bedroom, the salamander is in the bathroom, and the newt is in the kitchen, and (2) the goldfish likes the aerating sea chest, the gourami likes the plastic algae, and the halibut likes the ceramic bell-diver.

Logical Reasoning

Remember what we said about visualization in our discussion of mathematical reasoning? Look how helpful it is in logical reasoning. These are fairly simple problems, but they'd be fairly difficult without those charts, wouldn't they?

And don't assume that charts are only for simple problems. In fact, problems like the ones we've been looking at can get very complicated, indeed, and it's a logic problem in itself just to figure out how to construct the chart to best solve them. If you enjoyed doing these, or if you just want more exercise in figuring them out, you might want to pick up a book of them. *The Dell Book of Logic Puzzles* is good for this purpose, and it even has easy, intermediate, and difficult sections.

Speaking of assumptions, here's something you should keep in mind when using logic. One of the biggest sources of logical error comes from making unwarranted assumptions, and doing logic puzzles will help you tune in to that problem, which we al. have, to some extent. When we discover a mistaken assumption in our everyday lives, it usually comes as something of a shock, and it's instructive to reflect on how many mistaken assumptions must still be residing around us, *never* to be discovered. It's a disquieting thought, isn't it?

Reading good detective mysteries is a great way to exercise your logical reasoning, and I highly recommend those by Agatha Christie and Arthur Conan Doyle. One of the best fictional portrayals of a logical character (well, one we'd like to have as a friend, anyway) is Sherlock Holmes, who used both overt clues and subtle ones to draw entirely logical, yet astounding conclusions, thus solving the crime in question.

Try watching one of the old black-and-white Sherlock Holmes (played by Basil Rathbone) films on television soon, and notice how Holmes makes his deductions. He observes his surroundings with extreme care—so extreme that sometimes he appears to be able to observe a single hair out of place on Watson's head and from that determine the whole course of the good doctor's morning. But it always turns out that Holmes isn't a fortune-teller; there are clues right in front of our eyes that *he* sees and *we* don't. If we watch the movie a second time, it seems so obvious in retrospect.

Which brings us to a very important suggestion about how to improve your logical reasoning—at work, at home, and in most other areas of your everyday life. Perhaps you noticed it was employed (in a strict way) in the logic problems you just solved. And this is it: Every time you obtain a new fact, go back over the entire problem again. Relationships that seemed innocent at first can "jump out at you" as worthy of further investigation the next time around. (And the time after that, too.)

Here are a few more exercises:

1. The symphony hall couldn't afford an exterminator, and during a particularly pleasant overture, four insects—an ant, a fly, a termite, and a cockroach—creep out from the woodwork to listen to a concert. They each sit atop their favorite instrument—a bass fiddle, a drum, a tuba, and a piano. Who is where?

A. The cockroach once tried to eat the insect on the drum.
B. The termite is afraid of the insect sitting on the tuba.
C. The ant, the termite, and the one on the piano are chums.
D. The ant dislikes string instruments.

	Ant	Fly	Termite	Cockroach
Bass fiddle				
Drum				
Tuba				
Piano				

2. The holiday season has arrived, and it's time to buy gifts. Your neighbors—the Poes, the Hitchcocks, the Addamses, and the Munsters—will each expect a suitable gift for their pets—a bat, a cobra, a Gila monster, and a tarantula. Who is whose?
A. The Hitchcocks are scared of Gila monsters.
B. The Poes and the Munsters have never met the family that owns the bat.
C. The Poes and the Hitchcocks are best friends and frequently exchange pets.
D. The family of the tarantula is feuding with the Addamses.

	Poes	Hitchcocks	Addamses	Munsters
Bat				
Cobra				
Gila monster				
Tarantula				

3. A tabloid runs a story about a man who picks up women—a typist, an accountant, an attorney, and a dictator—and turns them into birds. Four birds are found fluttering about his house—a hummingbird, a finch, a parakeet, and a vulture. Who was what?
A. The finch likes the dictator and the hummingbird.
B. The typist once saw the vulture professionally.
C. The vulture doesn't know the accountant or the dictator.
D. The hummingbird is fighting with the attorney.

	Typist	Accountant	Attorney	Dictator
Hummingbird				
Finch				
Parakeet				
Vulture				

Here are the answers: (1) The ant is on the drum, the fly is on the piano, the termite is on the bass fiddle, and the cockroach is on the tuba, (2) the Poes own the cobra, the Hitchcocks own the tarantula, the Addamses own the bat, and the Munsters own the Gila monster, and (3) the typist is the hummingbird, the accountant is the finch, the attorney is the vulture, and the dictator is the parakeet.

Logic has an illogical reputation. Many people view a logical mind almost as a weakness instead of the great strength it is, and that's enormously detrimental to those people. They do everything straight from the heart—which is fine when it comes to puppies, paintings, and poetry, but is dangerously weak when it comes to curing the sick, landing on the moon, or winning a war.

Using logic doesn't mean that you need to, or should, alter your personality. It simply means that you can reason more effectively, making life a little, or a lot, easier for yourself and probably for those around you, too. In fact, logic is an important part of every chapter of this book, even though we don't mention it specifically elsewhere. Although we might see the use of logic as a self-contained process, it is used in nearly all intellectual functions.

There can be logic problems *within* logic problems, too, and it can all be incredibly complex, sometimes resulting in such errors as circular reasoning, specious reasoning, and sophistry. Major theories in science can rest innocently and uneasily on logic that may be filled with fact but is so far removed from direct human comprehension—certain areas of theoretical physics, for instance—that no one knows it until an event comes along that proves the theory utterly false. And even then, old theories die hard, especially when they've been well accepted by the academic community. People just *hate* to be wrong.

BOOK SEVEN

Ingenuity

Insight

Try this true/false quiz to learn a little more about your powers of insight.

1. I never think about how I'm going to approach something ahead of time. I just start, and whatever happens, happens. And most of the time, I don't like what happens.
2. I like the trial-and-error approach best. I have a lot of error, all right, but I do get there eventually.
3. I like to plan everything in excruciating detail. This usually works, although not without a lot of effort.
4. Solutions to problems occasionally just flash in my mind like a light bulb turning on. (Aha!)
5. Whenever I come upon a tough problem, I put it on the back burner, where it keeps cooking with all the rest of the problems. Then I go on to other things, and more often than not, problems seem to almost solve themselves when I get back to them.

An answer of "true" to numbers 1, 2, and 3 is normal, although number 2 probably describes the most efficient method of solving a problem. A "true" to number 4 shows that you have moments of real insight, and a "true" to number 5 shows that you already know how to go about getting more. Regardless, read on.

Here are some exercises, all taken from the physical sciences, subjects in which insight has played an essential role.

The following are some facts about astronomy:

GIVEN: The Earth was assumed to be flat until the time of the ancient Greeks Pythagoras and Aristotle, the latter of whom noted that the shadow of the Earth that falls on the moon during an eclipse of the moon is curved. This view was not popularly accepted for many years, however, and modern astronomy wasn't launched until the sixteenth century—when Copernicus proposed that the Earth revolves around the sun, and not vice versa. A half-century later, Galileo's newly invented telescope proved Copernicus correct, but the Church threatened Galileo with torture if he didn't rescind his views. (He did.)

GIVEN: Ancient scientists believed that the Earth was the largest object in the universe. Today we know that's far from the case. Our planet is only the fifth-largest in the Solar System. Jupiter, Saturn, Neptune, and Uranus are ranked numbers one through four.

GIVEN: Outer space is so vast that the units of distance we use on Earth aren't large enough to be useful there. Instead, astronomers used the "light-year," which is the distance light travels in a year. Because light travels about 186,282 miles per second in the near-vacuum of space, the distance it can go in a year is about 5.88 trillion miles. (As a comparison, the speed of sound, which is incapable of traveling in a vacuum, is only 1,128 feet per second.) But the most modern measure of distance in space is called the parsec, equivalent to 3.26 light-years.

Now's the time to stretch your powers of insight beyond what you've already read. Given the above as facts, which of the following statements are likely to be true?

1. Although the Church threatened Galileo with torture, they defended the proposals of Copernicus.
2. While ancient scientists mistakenly thought the Earth was the largest planet, it was obvious to them that the sun was far larger than the Earth.
3. A light-year is a measure of time.
4. The speed of sound is impractical for measuring distance in space.

Here are the answers: (1) False, (2) False, (3) False, and (4) True.

Here are some facts from meteorology and the earth sciences:

GIVEN: The Earth's atmosphere—carbon dioxide, in particular—acts like a glass blanket, transmitting visible light coming in from the sun but preventing the infrared radiation from dispersing back throughout space. This is called the "greenhouse effect."

GIVEN: Ultraviolet radiation bombarding the Earth from the sun is what causes sunburn and even skin cancer. Most of the radiation, however, is absorbed by the atmosphere's layer of ozone, the most chemically activ form of oxygen. Chlorofluorocarbons (such as aerosols and refrigerants), however, react with the ozone molecules and convert them into ordinary oxygen molecules.

GIVEN: The Earth is composed of layers. The outer shell, called the "crust," consists of the continents and the ocean basins. This crust is broken into vast "plates" that slide slowly within the middle shell and can diverge (causing rifts where new crust forms from volcanoes) or converge (where crust is destroyed and continents crumple). Where plates only scrape against each other, a fault zone is formed, and violent earthquakes can result.

Which of the following statements are likely to be true?

1. Without carbon dioxide in the atmosphere, the Earth would be very cold.
2. The term "greenhouse effect" originates in agricultural technique.
3. Although chlorofluorocarbons damage the ozone layer, they are helpful in that they convert ozone into breathable oxygen.
4. It would be good to have more ozone near the surface of the Earth.
5. The motion of the Earth's plates can cause entire continents to move toward each other and apart from each other.
6. Mountains are formed where the Earth's plates converge.

Here are the answers: (1) True, (2) True, (3) False, (4) False, (5) True, and (6) True.

The trickiest statement was number 4. It seems like an extension of the given fact, but there's no supporting logical bridge. Actually, ozone is a noxious pollutant near the Earth's surface.

Insight

What is insight? Is it something esoteric, achieved only by scientists who have managed to grasp a truly "revolutionary" understanding, such as the Earth revolving around the sun rather than the other way around? (Forgive us. We seldom have such a good opportunity for such a bad pun!) Not at all. Insight is nothing more than the "Aha!" principle—that deliciously satisfying flash of understanding that comes to us "out of the blue."

The history of science is full of stories of such unexpected insights. Remember Archimedes, the legendary Greek mathematician and physicist? As he lowered himself into a bath, he realized that a given weight of gold would displace less water than an equal weight of silver, which is less dense than gold. This was the fellow who then was supposed to have run home naked, shouting, "Eureka! Eureka!"—"I have found it! I have found it!"—thus lowering himself still further. (Oops. We promise that'll be the last time.)

But how about insight in everyday life? Well, a good example is suddenly realizing why your checkbook won't balance. You don't know quite how, and you don't know quite why, but suddenly you "think of something," and that turns out to be it. Which brings us to an important point—and one of the ways to have insight a little more often. You need to try more ideas. (The way you try balancing your checking account.) The more ideas you have, of course, the more of them that will be wrong. But who really cares about how many times Archimedes got it all wrong beforehand? Those are the times you don't hear about, but they're there, all right.

Trying new ideas is easy, but many people don't—mainly for two reasons: They don't think they're creative enough, and they don't have the necessary self-confidence. Of those two, the creative mind is *far* easier to get. Take a look back at those statements that were likely to follow from the "given" ones. The ones that were true are known facts these days, but it wasn't always that way. If *you* had thought of one of them, you would have had that significant insight yourself—like Copernicus. But most folks don't have the kind of self-confidence it takes to consider themselves capable of such things. And that's a pervasive attitude that reaches into every corner of our lives, from figuring out how to get the new sofa through the front door to restructuring an unprofitable business.

So try a little harder and much more often. You lack self-confidence? Okay. Don't worry about it. You don't have to tell anyone you're trying. Just go ahead and do it.

As you're reading through the coming exercises, try to keep insight in mind. You don't need to come up with anything on your own—we'll still give you the true/false questions that follow—but you should just begin to get used to thinking of the "givens" as *tools,* not conclusions. It's one of the most important ways to achieve insight. That is, to develop an active, inquiring mind. When you look up at the moon and the stars, it's fine just to take in that dazzling celestial spectacle, and it's also fine to think, "What if . . . ?"

Here are more exercises, these from Newtonian physics:

GIVEN: Newton's First Law defines "inertia," the tendency of an object to continue to do what it is already doing until acted upon by a "force," whatever compels it to do otherwise.

GIVEN: Newton's Second Law states that "force equals mass times acceleration," defining the relationship between an object's bulk, its acceleration, and any forces involved.

GIVEN: Newton's Third Law states that every action has an equal and opposite reaction. As you sit in a chair reading this book, the chair exerts an equal force upward on you.

GIVEN: Newton's Law of Universal Gravitation states that between any two objects there is a force of attraction, the strength of which is based on the mass of each object and how far apart they are. However, it is such a weak force, comparatively speaking, that it only becomes significant on a planetary scale.

Which of the below statements are likely to be true?

1. If you were traveling in a train, and the train were to stop abruptly, you would slowly stop with it.
2. The greater the force, the greater the mass.
3. When you slam down a telephone receiver, an equal force is exerted on the receiver by the phone cradle.
4. A man weighing one-thousand pounds can draw objects toward him.

Here are the answers: (1) False, (2) False, according to Newton, but Einstein refined the subject, (3) True, and (4) False, other than food.

These exercises are from the subject of chemistry:

GIVEN: The atom is the basic building block of all matter, and it is composed largely of three types of particles: protons, neutrons, and electrons. Varying combinations of these particles is what makes one substance differ from another. Materials containing only one kind of atom are called elements, and they include oxygen, mercury, and gold.

GIVEN: A molecule is the smallest amount of any chemical substance.

A few molecules contain only one atom, but most contain two or more bound together. A compound (formed by chemical reaction) consists of molecules composed of the atoms (or ions) of two or more different elements. A mixture (formed simply by physical combination) consists of two or more elements or compounds.

GIVEN: All matter has three familiar states: solid (the coolest state), liquid (the state that occurs when a solid melts), and gas (the state that occurs when a liquid boils).

Which of the following are likely to be true?

1. Water (H_2O) is an element.
2. Water is a compound.
3. Dishwater is a mixture.
4. If ozone got cold enough, it could turn into a solid.
5. If a sunbather got hot enough, he could turn into a gas.

Here are the answers: (1) False, (2) True, (3) True, (4) True, and (5) True. (But we know you'd put up the beach umbrella first.)

So now you know. There is nothing mystical about insight, and it is not the province of someone with far greater arcane knowledge than you'll ever possess (or want to, for that matter). In short, insight is simply "speed logic." It's being able to think, "Well, if A is true and B is true, then—hey!—C must be true!," without stopping to notice the steps.

But people differ in the way they get their insights. Some do their best thinking in the morning, when they're most rested, and others do it late at night, when you'd think they'd be their most tired. And then there are plenty of anecdotes about people who've had insights come to them in dreams. (And some of them may even be true.) For example, consider the experience of Friedrich August Kekulé, the German chemist who laid the foundation for the structural theory of organic chemistry. Back in 1865, Professor Kekulé dreamed of the benzene molecule as a snake swallowing its own tail while whirling in a circle (the snake, that is, not Professor Kekulé). From that dream arose the concept of the six-carbon benzene ring, and organic chemistry was newly understood.

Notwithstanding the fact that you wouldn't *want* dreams like Professor Kekulé's—I prefer flying, myself—you shouldn't be disappointed if all your insights are on a small scale. It's a start. And the more you practice, the better you'll get. Besides, insights can add up, and numerous small but excellent insights can someday provide a staircase for you to reach a very grand conclusion, indeed.

Ingenuity

Creativity

How creative are you? Take this true/false quiz and find out:

1. The clothes hanging in my closet are grouped in "out-fits" that go together.
2. The clothes in my closet are grouped by function, such as jackets all together, pants all together, or skirts all together.
3. The clothes in my closet are in no particular order, and are on the floor as often as they are on hangers.
4. I often try to devise new and unusual ways of solving problems.
5. I don't usually try to find creative solutions, but they seem to happen now and then anyway.

A "true" to number 1 indicates a lack of creativity, but a "true" to number 2 indicates a willingness to try new combinations. A "true" to number 3, though, shows a lack of discipline, which isn't synonymous with creativity, a skill that must be harnessed to be used productively. A "true" to number 4? Being different for the sake of being different is more eccentric than creative, but a "true" to number 5 shows you're already quite successful.

Here are some exercises to expand your ability to think creatively. Don't be concerned with "right" answers. Just answer as imaginatively as possible within the limits of your present knowledge. That is, don't violate any scientific principles that you already know, but don't worry about any of the rest of them. Look back at the facts presented in the first half of this chapter if you need to refresh your memory. We'll start with astronomy again:

1. Imagine that a time traveler has arrived from the year 500 B.C., and he believes that the Earth is flat. Without using a telescope, how would you convince him otherwise?

2. This same time traveler, his knowledge of the cosmos suddenly plunged into doubt, asks if the Earth is still considered the largest object in the universe. Again, without a telescope, how would you show him that it isn't?

3. Your time traveler is reeling, and you haven't even shown him your VCR. You decide to go a step further and tell him that light travels much faster than sound. He asks how anyone would know this. How could you persuade him?

There are no black-and-white, right-and-wrong answers here. The whole point was to exercise your imagination, so don't concern yourself with a score. You might have solved the first and second problems by giving the time traveler a ride on a space shuttle for a better view; in the third case, you might have observed a thunderstorm closely, noting that we hear the thunder after we see the lightning. (Not that they didn't observe storms in 500 B.C., but maybe our time traveler was afraid of thunder.)

Here are some exercises that use meteorology and earth sciences:

1. You travel to the future yourself. The fears of global warming have turned out to be justified, and the problem is serious. The polar icecaps are beginning to melt. How would you reduce the concentration of carbon dioxide in the atmosphere?

2. The ozone layer now resembles a sieve more than a blanket, and ultraviolet radiation has reached a critical level. How would you try to bring back the old days?

3. Take a giant leap into the far future. The continents have been shifting on the Earth's sliding plates and have slowly converged into one vast landmass. How have political systems accommodated to the change?

Okay, not even our world leaders have solved these problems, but since when has mental fitness been a prerequisite for being a world leader?! To solve the first problem, you might have suggested an outright ban on the burning of fossil fuel or an effort to frighten the world's plant life into hyperventilation. (Look, it's creative, isn't it?) To solve the second problem, you might have imagined a pipeline from polluted areas to send "bad" ozone back up to where it belongs, making it "good" again. (Or you might even have argued—weakly, admittedly—that the greenhouse effect couldn't be that bad if the ozone layer is that frayed.) To answer the third question, you might have theorized anything from world government to perpetual world war.

Creativity

As the British author Arthur Koestler once said, "Creativity in science could be described as the act of putting two and two together to make five." That's the sort of creativity we're seeking in this "ingenuity" chapter, and it applies to artistic endeavors, as well. It's the act of putting Beethoven and a piano together to make the *Moonlight* Sonata.

There are many who continually astound us with their bold imaginations—great cosmologists, great artists, great composers (and just about any attorney). And then there are children, of course, who have the ability to easily disassociate themselves from reality and readily imagine the unimaginable. We can learn a lesson from them. Why are children so creative? *Because they're uneducated.* They haven't been told what's "right" and what's "wrong," so their minds can run free. Not that education can be taken lightly. But neither should it be taken uncritically.

For a more practical example, let's suppose that cosmologists, astronomers, and physicists alike are taught that the null result of the Michelson-Morley experiment is unambiguous, and that this led to Einstein's proposal that the speed of light is a universal constant (among other things), ergo that the special theory of relativity is correct and certainly the governing principle of the way things work. Well, I hope it's correct, because if it isn't, we will have utterly stifled scientific progress in this area for nearly a century. (So far.)

Unless you're an aspiring Picasso, unbridled creativity won't do much good for you or for anyone else. But channeled into your professional and/or personal goals, it can unleash your potential for growth. To help unlock and nurture your natural creativity, try a few of these suggestions:

Are there any good art museums around where you live? Go visit one and walk through every room—whether you think you're interested in what's in a particular room or not. And inspect every work of art as if it were one of your favorites.

Are there any plays in town? Look through the newspaper and mark off any that you think you'd especially like. Then forget about those, and go to see all the *other* ones.

Do you have any new neighbors or co-workers who seem foreign to you? (That is, people of different nationalities or ethnic backgrounds.) Make friends, and at the first opportunity, tell them about a problem you've had and ask how they might go about solving it. You may be surprised.

Have you ever invented anything? Try. Go to any well-stocked hardware store and look through the nuts-and-bolts sort of aisles. (Stay away from anything already built.) Take your time. Buy little samplings of anything that appeals to you, then take it home and put together anything that has some sort of household function, however insignificant. Creativity isn't just the domain of the artist; it's a necessary part of every independent life.

Back to more exercises. Here are some from Newtonian physics:

1. **Let's say you're playing billiards. Using any number of balls, how would you demonstrate Newton's First Law, which states that an object will tend to continue to do what it is already doing until something else compels it to do otherwise?**
2. **Consider Newton's Second Law, defining the relationship between an object's bulk, its acceleration, and any forces involved. How would you use any objects on hand to demonstrate that these factors are indeed related?**
3. **And how would you demonstrate Newton's Third Law, namely, that every action has an equal and opposite reaction?**
4. **Name two objects in the room that would generate a force of attraction on any other object.**

To demonstrate the First Law, any bank shot would do, even (if you're like me) witnessing the ball rebound from the far wall. To demonstrate the Second Law, you could have shown that the more forcefully you shoot the cue ball, the faster it will travel and the harder it will hit another ball, the table, or your playing partner. A smaller ball would require less force to travel at the same speed.

To demonstrate the Third Law, you could have placed several balls together in perfect alignment exactly parallel to the table sides, shot the also-perfectly-aligned cue ball at one end, watched the force subtly ripple through the row, sending off the last ball in line to carom off the table, heading straight back to hit the second-last ball in line, which would then send a like force rippling back in the other direction through the row, again sending off the last ball to repeat the whole process until it all came to a gradual halt due to the intervention of friction. (It might not have worked *quite* that way in real life, we know.)

The fourth was a trick question. *Any* object exerts an attractive force, however weak, on any other object, so anything you named, including the cue ball, the chalk, or the heavily tattooed man named "Rocky," is correct. Award yourself innumerable points.

And now we arrive at chemistry again:

1. Let's say you're cooking a nice Thanksgiving dinner for your new in-laws. As you're preparing the appetizers, your father-in-law, testing your intelligence, asks you to explain what atoms are. Using any materials on hand, how would you demonstrate, at least theoretically, that the atom is the basic building block of all matter?
2. While the turkey is roasting, you're in the midst of making a pumpkin pie for dessert. Your dear father-in-law, continuing to test your intelligence, asks you to tell him the difference between a compound and a mixture. Again, using any materials on hand, how would you demonstrate the difference?
3. Meanwhile, your mother-in-law has been keeping a running commentary on every move you make. If you wanted to turn her into a gas, how would you go about it?

To the first question, you could have suggested something akin to what the ancient Greek philosopher Democritus argued: With a Perfect Knife (a hypothetical cutting instrument that would make a fortune with late-night television advertising), take a chunk of cheese and cut off a piece of it. Cut a piece off that piece, then cut another piece off *that* piece, and so on until even your Perfect Knife can't cut any more pieces off. You now have in your hand the smallest particle of cheese that exists: a "cheese atom," if cheese were an element. (All you need now is a "wine atom" to go with it.)

To answer the second question, you could have shown your father-in-law some granulated sugar and told him that sugar is a compound, made of three different elements (carbon, hydrogen, and oxygen) that are bound together chemically. Then you could show him the pumpkin filling itself and tell him that it's a mixture. Although its ingredients (sugar, eggs, pumpkin, etc.) have been physically combined, they aren't actually bound together chemically and could be separated.

For the third problem, we'll leave the specifics to your imagination, but any method you use would have to involve heating her to a very high temperature!

How did you do? Creativity is essential to the scientist as well as to the artist. While van Gogh dazzles us with a stunning vision of the night sky, the scientist dazzles us by presenting the facts about what is actually going on up there.

But creativity is not reserved for geniuses. It's employed by everyone and is a necessary element for survival. The only thing that stifles it is fear—the fear of independence. Ptolemy believed that the Earth was the center of our solar system. What if Copernicus had believed him, instead of showing that the planets moved in circular orbits around the sun? And what if Kepler had believed Copernicus, instead of showing that the planets moved in elliptical orbits around the sun? And what if physicists all believe Einstein without question?

Have you heard of the national Invent America! student-invention competition, sponsored and administered by the United States Patent Model Foundation? When I was a judge, I inspected everything from year-round sleds to paint-roller washers to twine-stapling guns to disappearing window screens—and these things were invented by grade-school kids! Creativity is more than finger-painting, and these young people are proving it.

Creativity is everything housed in Chicago's Museum of Science and Industry. It's everything in the National Air and Space Museum, the National Gallery of Art, the National Museum of History and Technology, and the Cooper-Hewitt Museum of Decorative Arts and Design, all parts of the Smithsonian Institution. It's everything in the Louvre in Paris and in the Vatican museums in Rome. It's everything at the National Aeronautics and Space Administration (NASA). And it's in every child.

Coded Information

Numerical

What do you know about codes and interpreting them?

1. I don't ever have to deal with codes. After all, I'm not James Bond, you know.
2. Interpreting codes? I can't even remember my *zip* code.
3. But I do sort of remember that the digits in my social security number are supposed to stand for something.
4. I can identify patterns in most areas of life.
5. I feel comfortable alone in foreign countries, even when I'm totally unfamiliar with the language.

If you answered "true" to number 1, you probably don't know the significance of learning how to "decode" information. (Yet.) It's not surprising; many people associate codes with secret decoder rings and espionage. In fact, it's a mental skill that can unlock the door to the world of science and understanding. Answers of "true" to number 2 and number 3 are normal. However, a "true" to number 4 is incompatible with a "false" to number 5. If you're able to identify patterns well, you'll handle most foreign countries with relative ease. Foreign ways, including foreign languages, are just coded expressions for some very ordinary stuff.

Here are some exercises, all relating to the subject of film, using examples that were both pioneering and influential. First, read each short description of the film. Then you'll be presented with a group of codes of these same descriptions. They will include the title, year, and director of the film as hints, and then you'll be asked to "decode" the description (without looking back, of course). The codes are different for each description. All the exercises will be about the same length, so time yourself on each one of them. Instead of measuring your ability with a score, your times will show you how much you're improving. (If you're really desperate, you can peek back at the description, but try not to do it often.) The "code keys" will be listed at the end of the exercises.

The first two films are very early experiments with the basic techniques of filmmaking:

A Trip to the Moon (1902—Georges Méliès). Méliès introduced the fade-in and fade-out, the "lap" dissolve, and stop-motion photography. He also focused on storylines, beginning the transformation of film from a documentary medium to a narrative one. (Not that anyone could mistake *A Trip to the Moon* for a documentary, though. At least not then.)

The Great Train Robbery (1903—Edwin S. Porter). Porter explored the potential of editing, including the use of stock footage, time-lapse photography, and innovative parallel action. Along with such "special effects" as hand-tinted smoke for the gunfights, *The Great Train Robbery* was enormously successful and led to the opening of movie theaters across the country.

Here are those same descriptions in code. Remember to time yourself while you work on breaking the codes.

1. *A Trip to the Moon* (1902—Georges Méliès). 13/5/12/9/5/19
    9/14/20/18/15/4/21/3/5/4 20/8/5 6/1/4/5-9/14 1/14/4
    6/1/4/5-15/21/20, 20/8/5 "12/1/16" 4/9/19/19/15/12/22/5,
    1/14/4 19/20/15/16-13/15/20/9/15/14
    16/8/15/20/15/7/18/1/16/8/25. 8/5 1/12/19/15
    6/15/3/21/19/5/4 15/14 19/20/15/18/25/12/9/14/5/19,
    2/5/7/9/14/14/9/14/7 20/8/5 20/18/1/14/19/6/15/18/13/1/20/9/15/14
    15/6 6/9/12/13 6/18/15/13 1 4/15/3/21/13/5/14/20/1/18/25
    13/5/4/9/21/13 20/15 1 14/1/18/18/1/20/9/22/5 15/14/5.
    (14/15/20 20/8/1/20 1/14/25/15/14/5 3/15/21/12/4
    13/9/19/20/1/11/5 *1 20/18/9/16 20/15 20/8/5
    13/15/15/14 6/15/18 1 4/15/3/21/13/5/14/20/1/18/25,*
    20/8/15/21/7/8. 1/20 12/5/1/19/20 14/15/20 20/8/5/14.)

2. *The Great Train Robbery* (1903—Edwin S. Porter).
11/12/9/7/22/9   22/3/11/15/12/9/22/23   7/19/22
11/12/7/22/13/7/18/26/15   12/21   22/23/18/7/18/13/20,
18/13/24/15/6/23/18/13/20   7/19/22   6/8/22   12/21
8/7/12/24/16   21/12/12/7/26/20/22,   7/18/14/22-
15/26/11/8/22   11/19/12/7/12/20/9/26/11/19/2,   26/13/23
18/13/13/12/5/26/7/18/5/22   11/26/9/26/15/15/22/15
26/24/7/18/12/13.   26/15/12/13/20   4/18/7/19   8/6/24/19
"8/11/22/24/18/26/15   22/21/21/22/24/7/8"   26/8   19/26/13/23-
7/18/13/7/22/23   8/14/12/16/22   21/12/9   7/19/22
20/6/13/21/18/20/19/7/8,   7/19/22   20/9/22/26/7
7/9/26/18/13   9/12/25/25/22/9/2   4/26/8
22/13/12/9/14/12/6/8/15/2   8/6/24/24/22/8/8/21/6/15
26/13/23   15/22/23   7/12   7/19/22   12/11/22/13/18/13/20
12/21   14/12/5/18/22   7/19/22/26/7/22/9/8 26/24/9/12/8/8
7/19/22   24/12/6/13/7/9/2.

These films pioneered the modern concept of narrative film:

Birth of a Nation (1915—D.W. Griffith). This Civil War epic changed the image of motion pictures forever as film moved from primitive to classical. Wildly controversial, it discarded stage-bound settings and moved further into the realm of broader realism with the use of symbolism. What the film lacked in political correctness, it made up for in technical achievement.

Battleship Potemkin (1925—Sergei Eisenstein). This masterpiece that represented the mutiny of the Russian battleship *Potemkin* ushered in an era of editing technique that used direct psychological stimulation instead of narrative flow to convey emotion to the audience. No one who saw the massacre of citizens on the Odessa steps will ever forget it.

And here are the same descriptions in code:

3. *Birth of a Nation* (1915—D. W. Griffith).   21/9/10/20
4/10/23/10/13   24/2/19   6/17/10/4   4/9/2/15/8/6/5   21/9/6
10/14/2/8/6   16/7   14/16/21/10/16/15   17/10/4/21/22/19/6/20
7/16/19/6/23/6/19 2/20   7/10/13/14   14/16/23/6/5   7/19/16/14
17/19/10/14/10/21/10/23/6   21/16   4/13/2/20/20/10/4/2/13.
24/10/13/5/13/26   4/16/15/21/19/16/23/6/19/20/10/2/13,   10/21
5/10/20/4/2/19/5/6/5   20/21/2/8/6-3/16/22/15/5
20/6/21/21/10/15/8/20   2/15/5   14/16/23/6/5
7/22/19/21/9/6/19   10/15/21/16   21/9/6   19/6/2/13/14
16/7   3/19/16/2/5/6/19   19/6/2/13/10/20/14   24/10/21/9
21/9/6   22/20/6   16/7   20/26/14/3/16/13/10/20/14.
24/9/2/21   21/9/6   7/10/13/14   13/2/4/12/6/5   10/15

17/16/13/10/21/10/4/2/13 4/16/19/19/6/4/21/15/6/20/20,
10/21 14/2/5/6 22/17 7/16/19 10/15 21/6/4/9/15/10/4/2/13
2/4/9/10/6/23/6/14/6/15/21.

4. *Battleship Potemkin* (1925—Sergei Eisenstein). 19/7/8/18
    12/0/18/19/4/17/15/8/4/2/4 19/7/0/19 17/4/15/17/4/18/4/ 3/19/4/3
    19/7/4 12/20/19/8/13/24 14/5 19/7/4 17/20/18/18/8/0/13
    1/0/19/19/11/4/18/7/8/15 15/14/19/4/12/10/8/13 20/18/7/4/17/4/3
    8/13 0/13 4/17/0 14/5 4/3/8/19/8/13/6 19/4/2/7/13/8/16/20/4
    19/7/0/19 20/18/8/3 3/8/17/2/19 15/18/24/2/7/14/11/14/6/8/2/0/11
    18/19/8/12/20/11/0/19/8/14/13 8/13/18/19/4/0/3 14/5
    13/0/17/17/0/19/8/21/4 5/11/14/22 19/14 2/14/13/21/4/24
    4/12/14/19/8/14/13 19/14 19/7/4 0/20/3/8/4/13/2/4. 13/14
    14/13/4 22/7/14 18/0/22 19/7/4 12/0/18/18/0/2/17/4 14/5
    2/8/19/8/25/4/13/18 14/13 19/7/4 14/3/4/18/18/0 18/19/4/15/18
    22/8/11/11 4/21/4/17 5/14/17/6/4/19 8/19.

Here are the "code keys": (1) Each number refers simply to each letter's numerical placement in the alphabet. That is, A = 1, B = 2, and Z = 26. (2) In this one, each number refers to each letter's placement in the alphabet, but in reverse order. That is, A = 26, B = 25, and Z = 1). (3) Here, each number refers to each letter's placement plus one. That is, A = 2, B = 3, and Z = 27. (4) And here, each number refers to each letter's placement minus one. That is, A = 0, B = 1, and Z = 25.

How did you do? As you progressed through the exercises, did you spend less time per film? (You might want to discount the first one.) If you did, that's exceptional. If you spent the same amount of time, that's still excellent, because the codes became harder. But if you spent more time as you went along, cheer up. That's very good. Just doing them all was the point, anyway. After all, what is your next-door neighbor doing? Watching television?

Numerical Codes

Unless you're a fan of breaking codes—and most people are not—you didn't go about this with a particular technique. That is, you gazed unhappily down at those lines for a moment and thought, "Oh well, maybe it won't be so bad," and you looked a little more, and then you noticed that, in some places, one number stood alone. As there are not many letters that stand alone as words, you knew it was an "a" or an "I." And then you noticed that the number was a "1," so you took a chance that the letter was an "a." And you were right. And then you got your feet wet and tolerated the next exercise far better, even though it was more difficult. And so on.

Professional decoders—we know you are not one of them, and that isn't the point of this chapter, anyway—start by considering the number of occurrences of a particular letter. If you add up all the "e's" in the *Gettysburg Address* and compare it to the number of "k's," for example, you'll see that not all letters are created equal. In fact, in the first sentence of this paragraph, there are 16 "e's," but only a single "k."

"E" is the most frequently used letter in the English language, followed by (surprise!) "t." Next in order in the high-frequency group are "a," "o," "n," "i," "r," "s," and (surprise again!) "h." The medium-frequency group consists of "d," "l," "u," "c," and "m," followed by the low-frequency group that consists of "p," "f," "y," "w," "g," "b," and "v." The rare-frequency group consists of "j," "k," "q," and "x," with "z" as the least used of all.

We're not going to make the codes very difficult in this chapter, because getting specialized decoding experience isn't the point here. Instead, we want you to exercise away that fogginess you feel when you first look at coded information and attempt to find patterns in it. And that's the key, of course—finding patterns. You'll want to look for combinations that frequently occur as a pair and for combinations that often form word endings, among other things.

Perhaps the best way to start decoding a long-enough passage in English is simply to count up the number of encoded letter (or number) frequencies and plug in the decoded letters in the appropriate places. (That is, if "r" occurs the most often, make that "e." If "l" occurs the next most often, make that "t.") Letter frequency is so constant within any one language that long-enough texts will all contain very similar proportions. Remember how we said the *Gettysburg Address* would contain a certain percentage of "e's" and another percentage of "k's"? An analysis of your last six letters to your mother will produce comparable percentages. (Well, maybe there'll be a few extra "I's" and "M's.")

To make messages even more obscure, cryptographers, or specialists in writing and deciphering coded messages, can encipher an encoded message, but this is done on purpose. What we'd like to exercise here, though, is your ability to "decode" the large number of innocent, ordinary patterns found in your life that aren't immediately apparent to understanding.

Now, back to some more exercises. (And remember to time yourself.)

These two films are very early horror movies:

The Cabinet of Dr. Caligari (1919—Robert Wiene). This is the film that established the genre, although less with horror than with general eerieness. Even the settings are oddly lit and twisted to represent more fully the disturbed and deranged mind of the narrator. The first successful portrayal of insanity, it brought Expressionism to "life."

Nosferatu: A Symphony of Horrors (1922—F. W. Murnau). This Expressionist film is the first and ultimate Dracula movie, and it still retains its ominous tone to this day, relying as it does upon camera angles and lighting rather than a big production budget. But go to see it with a sophisticated crowd. The depth of its sinister visual images causes some people to giggle.

Again, here are those descriptions in code:

1. *The Cabinet of Dr. Caligari* (1919—Robert Wiene). 40/16/18/38
   18/38   40/16/10   12/18/24/26   40/16/2/40
   10/38/40/2/4/24/18/38/16/10/8   40/16/10   14/10/28/36/10,
   2/24/40/16/30/42/14/16   24/10/38/38   46/18/40/16
   16/30/36/36/30/36   40/16/2/28   46/18/40/16   14/10/28/10/36/2/24
   10/10/36/18/10/28/10/38/38.   10/44/10/28   40/16/10
   38/10/40/40/18/28/14/38   2/36/10   30/8/8/24/50   24/18/40
   2/28/8   40/46/18/38/40/10/8   40/30   36/10/32/36/10/38/10/28/40
   26/30/36/10   12/42/24/24/50   40/16/10   8/18/38/40/42/36/4/10/8
   2/28/8   8/10/36/2/28/14/10/8   26/18/28/8   30/12   40/16/10
   28/2/36/36/2/40/30/36.   40/16/10   12/18/36/38/40
   38/42/6/6/10/38/38/12/42/24   32/30/36/40/36/2/50/2/24   30/12
   18/28/38/2/28/18/40/50,   18/40   4/36/30/42/14/16/40
   10/48/32/36/10/38/38/18/30/28/18/38/26   40/30   "24/18/12/10."

2. *Nosferatu: A Symphony of Horrors* (1922—F. W. Murnau).
   41/17/19/39   11/49/33/37/11/39/39/19/31/29/19/39/41   13/19/25/27
   19/39   41/17/11   13/19/37/39/41   3/29/9   43/25/41/19/27/3/41/11
   9/37/3/7/43/25/3   27/31/45/19/11,   3/29/9   19/41   39/41/19/25/25
   37/11/41/3/19/29/39   19/41/39   31/27/19/29/31/43/39   41/31/29/11
   41/31   41/17/19/39   9/3/51,   37/11/25/51/19/29/15   3/39   19/41
   9/31/11/39   43/33/31/29   7/3/27/11/37/3   3/29/15/25/11/39   3/29/9

25/19/15/17/41/19/29/15 37/3/41/17/11/37 41/17/3/29 3 5/19/15
33/37/31/9/43/7/41/19/31/29   5/43/9/15/11/41.   5/43/41   15/31
41/31   39/11/11   19/41   47/19/41/17   3
39/31/33/17/19/39/41/19/7/3/41/11/9   7/37/31/47/9.   41/17/11
9/11/33/41/17   31/13   19/41/39   39/19/29/19/39/41/11/37
45/19/39/43/3/25   19/27/3/15/11/39   7/3/43/39/11/39   39/31/27/11
33/11/31/33/25/11   41/31   15/19/15/15/25/11.

And here are two classic comedies:

The Gold Rush (1925—Charlie Chaplin). Chaplin became the first international movie star, and his "little tramp" character inspired generations of comic filmmakers. Jokes now so standard they seem almost trite suddenly come alive again when you see this movie—including the bear chase, the cabin teetering on the edge of a cliff, and the eating of the shoe.

The General (1925—Buster Keaton). Sometimes known as the "other" great comic epic, this priceless film is based on a real incident in the Civil War. Although a veritable showcase for Keaton's use of his "trajectory" device—a protracted series of dramatically linked sight gags—this film manages to be hilarious without being ridiculous.

And here are those descriptions in code:

3. *The Gold Rush* (1925—Charlie Chaplin). 5/15/1/31/23/17/27
   3/9/5/1/25/9   39/15/9   11/17/35/37/39
   17/27/39/9/35/27/1/39/17/29/27/1/23   25/29/43/17/9   37/39/1/35,
   1/27/7   15/17/37   "23/17/39/39/23/9   39/35/1/25/31"
   5/15/1/35/1/5/39/9/35   17/27/37/31/17/35/9/7
   13/9/27/9/35/1/39/17/29/27/37   29/11   5/29/25/17/5
   11/17/23/25/25/1/21/9/35/37.   19/29/21/9/37   27/29/45   37/29
   37/39/1/27/7/1/35/7   39/15/9/49   37/9/9/25
   1/23/25/29/37/39   39/35/17/39/9   37/41/7/7/9/27/23/49   5/29/25/9
   1/23/17/43/9   1/13/1/17/27   45/15/9/27   49/29/41   37/9/9
   39/15/17/37   25/29/43/17/9—17/27/5/23/41/7/17/27/13   39/15/9
   3/9/1/35   5/15/1/37/9, 39/15/9   5/1/3/17/27   39/9/9/39/9/35/17/27/13
   29/27   39/15/9   9/7/13/9   29/11   1   5/23/17/11/11,   1/27/7
   39/15/9   9/1/39/17/27/13   29/11   39/15/9   37/15/29/9.

4. *The General* (1925—Buster Keaton).
   43/35/31/15/45/23/31/15/43 27/33/35/51/33   7/43   45/21/15
   "35/45/21/15/41"   19/41/15/7/45   11/35/31/23/11   15/37/23/11,
   45/21/23/43   37/41/23/11/15/29/15/43/43   17/23/29/31   23/43
   9/7/43/15/13   35/33   7   41/15/7/29   23/33/11/23/13/15/33/45
   23/33   45/21/15   11/23/49/23/29   51/7/41.   7/29/45/21/35/47/19/21

7 49/15/41/23/45/7/9/29/15 43/21/35/51/11/7/43/15 17/35/41
27/15/7/45/35/33/'43 47/43/15 35/17 21/23/43
"45/41/7/25/15/11/45/35/41/55" 13/15/49/23/11/15—7
37/41/35/45/41/7/11/45/15/13 43/15/41/23/15/43 35/17
13/41/7/31/7/45/23/11/7/29/29/55 29/23/33/27/15/13
43/23/19/21/45 19/7/19/43—45/21/23/43 17/23/29/31
31/7/33/7/19/15/43 45/35 9/15 21/23/29/7/41/23/35/47/43
51/23/45/21/35/47/45 9/15/23/33/19
41/23/13/23/11/47/29/35/47/43.

And here are the "code keys" for the second group of films: (1) Each number refers simply to each letter's numerical placement in the alphabet times two. That is, A = 2, B = 4, and Z = 52. (2) In this one each number refers to each letter's placement in the alphabet times two, then plus one. That is, A = 3, B = 5, and Z = 53. (3) Here, each number refers to each letter's placement times two, then minus one. That is, A = 1, B = 3, and Z = 51. (4) And here, each number refers to each letter's placement times two, then plus five. That is, A = 7, B = 9, and Z = 57.

Interesting, isn't it? Now that you know the answers, you know that those were very simple codes. Then why did they seem so hard when you first looked at them? Some of you may have been so intimidated that you didn't even try them. But here's the point: This chapter has little to do with actual cryptography, although cryptography certainly has always had fascinating historical and political implications. For example, the coded messages sent by Mary, Queen of Scots, in 1586, were cracked to reveal her complicity in a plot to assassinate Queen Elizabeth I of England, leading ultimately to Mary's beheading. And then there was the decoding of the Zimmermann telegram in 1917, in which the German Kaiser's foreign minister offered to return to Mexico its "lost" territory of Arizona, New Mexico, and Texas in return for Mexico's declaring war on the United States.

But we're interested in the "coded" information in everyday life, the patterns of everything from clouds in the sky to the way two lovers communicate across a crowded room. A couple of weeks ago, I was having lunch with a friend, and we amused ourselves for a moment by observing how everyone seemed to know everyone else at this restaurant, a favorite for New Yorkers in the publishing business, and we talked about whether people should greet each other with a handshake or a kiss on the cheek. "As long as you're consistent, you're safe," he said with a smile. "Just think about what it looks like when a woman passes several men on her way out, and she kisses them all on the cheek except for one particular guy, who suddenly gets a handshake."

So this book's point in exercising with code-breaking is to help enhance your ability to "make sense out of nonsense," to see the meaningful patterns that are lying right in front of you, patterns that are bursting with information but disguised behind their unfamiliar elements. Code-breaking has something in common with learning how to read. It's a slow process, but just as a literate person appears very intelligent and understanding to an illiterate one, so too will you be more perceptive, more perspicacious when you develop the skill of deciphering patterns more broadly in life.

Coded Information

Alphabetical

How do you feel about your "decoding" or pattern recognition ability now?

1. I'm relieved to see the word "alphabetical" on this half of the chapter. Those numerical codes looked *terrible*.
2. Then again, maybe I have an unpleasant surprise in store.
3. I understand the reason for strengthening the skill of pattern recognition, but I sure don't understand why those simple codes were so hard.
4. Now that I've survived that last section, I'm sending my resumé to the CIA.
5. I'm seriously considering skipping to the next chapter and putting this whole embarrassing episode behind me.

If you answered "true" to number 1, you should have answered "true" to number 2 also. There's no reason to think alphabetical codes will be easier. A "true" to number 3 is normal, but a "true" to number 4 isn't. (My assistant wrote that one, and I think he's trying to tell me something!) But if you answered "true" to number 5, wait! Think of how g-u-i-l-t-y you'll feel. How g-u-i-l-t-y. Besides, we're going to become very witty and charming in this chapter.

Here are more exercises on the subject of film.

The following are two motion pictures that created genres still with us today:

Nanook of the North (1922—Robert Flaherty). This "narrative documentary" about a family of Eskimos living in the frozen Canadian Arctic exposed audiences to an exotic location for the first time, and they were riveted by it. Although the lives of the Eskimos were scripted for the camera, the story attempted to portray them as realistically as a documentary.

Metropolis (1926—Fritz Lang). This "science fiction" film presented the first frightening vision of the totalitarian nightmare society so beloved by the intellectual pessimists of this world. Especially noticeable is the way hundreds of extras were carefully coordinated to function more as scenery than as people.

Here are the encoded descriptions of the films. Don't forget to time yourself on each one:

1. *Nanook of the North* (1922—Robert Flaherty). UIJT "OBSSBUJWF EPDVNFOUBSZ" BCPVU B GBNJMZ PG FTLJNPT MJWJOH JO UIF GSPAFO DBOBEJBO BSDUJD FYQPTFE BVEJFODFT UP BO FYPUJD MPDBUJPO GPS UIF GJSTU UJNF, BOE UIFZ XFSF SJWFUFE CZ JU. BMUIPVHI UIF MJWFT PG UIF FTLJNPT XFSF TDSJQUFE GPS UIF DBNFSB, UIF TUPSZ BUUFNQUFE UP QPSUSBZ UIFN BT SFBMJTUJDBMMZ BT B EPDVNFOUBSZ.

2. *Metropolis* (1926—Fritz Lang). SGHR "RBHDMBD EHBSHNM" EHKL OQDRDMSDC SGD EHQRS EQHFGSDMHMF UHRHNM NE SGD SNSZKHSZQHZM MHFGSLZQD RNBHDSX RN ADKNUDC AX SGD HMSDKKDBSTZK ODRRHLHRSR NE SGHR VNQKC. DRODBHZKKX MNSHBDZAKD HR SGD VZX GTMCQDCR NE DWSQZR VDQD BZQDETKKX BNNQCHMZSDC SN ETMBSHNM LNQD ZR RBDMDQX SGZM ZR ODNOKD.

Here are two classic movies people in the nineteen-twenties and thirties were talking about—and talking *in*. Both were among the earliest, most successful experiments with the "talkies":

The Jazz Singer (1927—Alan Crosland). This was the first successful "talking" picture, although it was more of a "singing" picture in reality. Not designed to have dialogue initially, Al Jolson's spontaneous lines between the songs wound up in the finished film and gave audiences the thrill of hearing "real" dialogue instead of canned performances.

All Quiet on the Western Front (1930—Lewis Milestone). This heart-rending, pacifist film was anything *but* quiet as it explored the potential of post-dubbing, or filming with a silent camera and adding sound later. An independent soundtrack was separately created and superimposed on the filmed image. The result was potent psychological impact.

Here are the encoded descriptions of those films:

3. *The Jazz Singer* (1927—Alan Crosland). VJKU YCU VJG HKTUV UWEEGUUHWN "VCNMKPI" RKEVWTG, CNVJQWIJ KV YCU OQTG QH C "UKPIKPI" RKEVWTG KP TGCNKVA. PQV FGUKIPGF VQ JCXG FKCNQIWG KPKVKCNNA, CN LQNUQP'U URQPVCPGQWU NKPGU DGVYGGP VJG UQPIU YQWPF WR KP VJG HKPKUJGF HKNO CPF ICXG CWFKGPEGU VJG VJTKNN QH JGCTKPI "TGCN" FKCNQIWG KPUVGCF QH ECPPGF RGTHQTOCPEGU.

4. *All Quiet on the Western Front* (1930—Lewis Milestone). RFGQ FCYPRPCLBGLE, NYAGDGQR DGJK UYQ YLWRFGLE *ZSR* OSGCR YQ GR CVNJMPCLB RFC NMRCLRGYJ MD NMQR-BSZZGLE, MP DGJKGLE UGRF Y QGJCLR AYKCPY YLB YBBGLE QMSLB JYRCP. YL GLBCNCLBCLR QMSLBRPYAI UYQ QCNYPYRCJW APCYRCB YLB QSNCPGKNMQCB ML RFC DGJKCB GKYEC. RFC PCQSJR UYQ NMRCLR NQWAFMJMEGAYJ GKNYAR.

Here are the "code keys": In all these, envision the alphabet as a snake swallowing its own tail. That is, the letter that precedes A is Z, and the letter that follows Z is A. (1) Each letter is simply replaced by the letter that follows it. That is, A = B, B = C, and Z = A. (2) Each letter is replaced by the letter that precedes it. That is, A = Z, B = A, anc Z = Y. (3) Each letter is replaced by the letter *after* the letter that follows it. That is, A = C, B = D, and Z = B. (4) Each letter is replaced by the letter *before* the letter that precedes it. That is, A = Y, B = Z, and Z = X.

Alphabetical Codes

How did you do? It's worth repeating—every code you decoded at all, no matter how much time you took to do it, is a great stride forward in exercising your mental skills. Maybe you can look at it like physical exercise. It's fine to do more repetitions and do them faster, too, but doing them at all is the main thing. And you've done that. Congratulations!

Surprising, isn't it? The numerical codes looked far harder than the alphabetical ones, but that was an illusion, and it illustrates our point. Unfamiliar elements make easy things look difficult and make difficult things look impossible. But the less you fear them, the better you'll be able to handle them. In fact, the numerical codes were *easier* than the alphabetical ones, and that's why we placed them first.

This is an interesting lesson in pattern recognition. Numbers aren't really unfamiliar. You're just not used to seeing them lined up like that. But we lined them up for you, so you at least knew they were codes. What if we hadn't done that? And what if no one does? That is, how many patterns in life are you missing because you're not paying attention to the subtleties?

Here's a pleasant way to exercise your "decoding" ability—or more accurately, your perspicuity. If possible, go out to see (or rent) some foreign films, but don't read the subtitles. (Not that it's all that easy to read them, anyway. Foreign films that take place in the snow or at the beach can be a real *visual* exercise.) Just listen to the dialogue and watch the action carefully. Make a special effort to understand what's going on. You'll notice that you'll feel lost at first because you've become so dependent (and reasonably, of course) on using language as a "decoder." You may not even improve much by the end of the film. But consider seeing the same film again sometime, and plenty of other films. See how your visual focus—or more accurately, your perspicuity—sharpens. You'll even learn quite a bit that's not contained in the subtitles. They're only a condensed version of what's being said anyway, and when you're busy reading them, you're missing much of what's happening on the screen. But remember: Don't just sit there and watch. You've got to try very hard to accomplish anything.

Here's another suggestion: Do you have a friend or a relative who speaks a foreign language? Ask him or her to speak to you in that language frequently. Grandparents take a special delight in doing this. You're not going to become fluent this way (unless you speak back, and often), but it's a good lesson in learning how to "decode" such things as attitude, body language, and the multitude of other nonverbal and verbal clues.

Now back to some more exercises. Here are three extremely popular movies that heralded the coming of the color film:

Snow White and the Seven Dwarfs (1937—Walt Disney). Some years earlier, Disney had created the first "animated musical," featuring a hitherto-unknown young mouse named Mickey. *Snow White* was the first in a long line of full-length, animated color features that made Disney's name synonymous with quality musical cartoons.

The Wizard of Oz (1939—Victor Fleming). This film began and ended in sepia, framing the most advanced and imaginative use of color to date and turning the fantasy of Oz into reality on the screen. Considered the first "integrated" musical, where production numbers played a real role in the narrative, its characters burst into song at every opportunity.

Gone with the Wind (1939—Victor Fleming). This Civil War romance was the second* most profitable release in the history of American film. We suspect you know the story, but as far as technical qualities are concerned, it was the first movie to use Technicolor's new, breakthrough film, which vastly improved color realization and increased the depth of focus.

(*And which was the first, you ask? Would you believe *Birth of a Nation*? No, we didn't think you would.)

Here are the above descriptions in code. Don't forget to time yourself:

5. *Snow White and the Seven Dwarfs* (1937—Walt Disney). HLNV BVZIH VZIORVI, WRHMVB SZW XIVZGVW GSV URIHG "ZMRNZGVW NFHRXZO," UVZGFIRMT Z SRGSVIGL-FMPMLDM BLFMT NLFHV MZNVW NRXPVB. *HMLD DSRGV* DZH GSV URIHG RM Z OLMT ORMV LU UFOO-OVMTGS, ZMRNZGVW XLOLI UVZGFIVH GSZG NZWV WRHMVB'H MZNV HBMLMBNLFH DRGS JFZORGB NFHRXZO XZIGLLMH.

6. *The Wizard of Oz* (1939—Victor Fleming). HTSI VSPO ZWUAN ANX WNXWX SN IWLSA, VJAOSNU HTW OMIH AXFANYWX ANX SOAUSNAHSFW GIW MV YMPMJ HM XAHW ANX HGJNSNU HTW VANHAIC MV MB SNHM JWAPSHC MN HTW IYJWWN. YMNISXWJWX HTW VSJIH "SNHWUJAHWX" OGISYAP, ETWJW LJMXGYHSMN NGOZWJI LPACWX A JWAP JMPW SN HTW NAJJAHSFW, SHI YTAJAYHWJI ZGJIH SNHM IMNU AH WFWJC MLLMJHGNSHC.

7. *Gone with the Wind* (1939—Victor Fleming). FRQG WQDQN CYH HKMYLWU CYG FRU GUWKLV MKGF JHKTQFYXNU HU-

NUYGU QL FRU RQGFKHA KT YMUHQWYL TQNM. CU GEGJUWF
AKE OLKC FRU GFKHA, XEF YG TYH YG FUWRLQWYN
IEYNQFQUG YHU WKLWUHLUV, QF CYG FRU TQHGF MKDQU FK
EGU FUWRLQWKNKH'G LUC, XHUYOFRHKESR TQNM, CRQWR
DYGFNA QMJHKDUV WKNKH HUYNQZYFQKL YLV QLWHUYGUV
FRU VUJRF KT TKWEG.

And here's one last title. It has been voted "the best film of all time"
again and again, nationally and internationally, despite the fact that it
was booed repeatedly at the Academy Awards the first year it was re-
leased. In fact, it was such a failure at the box office that Hollywood
never again trusted its director with complete control. It didn't begin to
achieve recognition until it started to play the art-house circuit in the
nineteen-fifties.

If you've seen this film and don't know what all the fuss is about, or
if you're new to film appreciation and are going to see it for the first
time soon, here's something to keep in mind. We, who have been in-
undated with casts of thousands and special effects that rival the birth
of the sun, have become blinded by modern pyrotechnics. Instead of
fireworks, try thinking of this film as a multifaceted, perfect little gem.

Citizen Kane (1940—Orson Welles). Loosely (and unflatteringly) based
on the life of William Randolph Hearst, whose suppression tactics made
it a box-office failure, *Kane* was radically experimental in nearly every
way. Its unprecedented depth of focus allowed simultaneous action in
the foreground and background, its mastery of the "long take" founded
the art of composing shots in such a way as to require minimal intra-
scene editing, and it demonstrated consummate skill with creative use
of soundtrack, overlapping dialogue, and flashback narrative technique.
As if that weren't enough, Welles played the lead.

Here is that description in code:

8. *Citizen Kane* (1940—Orson Welles). DAELEHT (DEY
   ALPSELLEWHGUON) ETNER EW TAH TFIS AE UQINHCE TEVITARR
   ANKCAB, HSALF DNAEUGOLAID GNIPPAL REVO KC A RTD-
   NUOSFO ESUEVIT, *AERC* HTI WLLIKSETA MMUSNOCDETAR TS
   NOMEDT IDNAG NIT. IDE ENECSARTNILAM INIME RI UQERO
   TSAYAWA HCUSNISTOHSG NISOPM OC FOT RAEHTDEDNU OFE
   KATGNOLEHT, FOY RETSAMS TI DNU "ORGK CABD" NADNUOR
   GER OFE HT NINOITCAS UOENA TL UMIS D EWO LL AS UCOFFOH
   TPEDDET NEDEC-ERPNU STIYAWY, REV EY LRAENNILATNE
   MIREPXEYLL ACIDA RSAW ENAKERUL IAF EC IFFOXOBATI,
   EDAMSCITCAT NOISSERP, PUS ESOHWTSRA EHHPLODNA

RMAILLIWF. OE FI LEHT NODES'A BYLGNI, RETTAL FNUDNA YLE SOOL.

Here are the "code keys." Envision the alphabet as *two* snakes swallowing their own tail but facing opposite ways:

```
A B C D E F G H I J K L M N O P Q R S T U V W X Y Z
Z Y X W V U T S R Q P O N M L K J I H G F E D C B A
```

(5) Each letter becomes the letter "across" from it. That is, A = Z, B = Y, and Z = A. (6) Each letter becomes the letter across and one to the left. That is, A = A (!), B = Z, and Z = B. (7) Each letter becomes the letter across and one to the right. That is, A = Y, B = X, and Z = Z (!). (8) The entire quotation is simply backward!

The mind is constantly decoding and coding information, making sense out of nonsense, and organizing it in accessible form. Your physician deciphers your pattern of symptoms and diagnoses your illness; your accountant deciphers your shoebox full of papers and makes out your tax return; your mother deciphers your telephone-answering pattern and realizes that you haven't been spending many weekends at home lately.

What does "decipher" mean, after all? It means to "decode," to interpret the "hidden" meaning in patterns, regardless of whether that pattern happens to be right in front of your nose. And the world is suffused with patterns "waiting" to be discovered, both mundane and exotic. Discovering patterns underlies the whole of scientific research. That is one of the uses to which people put data. They study it, try to find patterns in it, and use them to construct keys to unlock the secrets of the universe. "Breaking" the genetic code, so to speak, unlocks the door to the information coded within the nucleotide sequences of DNA and RNA, which delineates the amino-acid sequence in the synthesis of proteins, and upon which all of heredity is based.

Hmm. We've just remembered that we said we were going to become very witty and charming in this chapter. You wouldn't settle for "apologetic," would you? (No, we didn't think you would.) Oh well, it's too late now.

Part Three

CONCRETE THINKING

BOOK NINE

Picture Completion

What's Wrong

Do you know when something's "just not right"?

1. Whenever my spouse says, "So, do you notice anything different about me?" I usually guess the wrong thing and feel silly afterward.
2. I guess it depends on whether I'm familiar with the subject. If I'm looking at a lawnmower, I'm not going to notice any problems unless it's in flames.
3. I'm not all that bad at spotting a real error, though.
4. I'm like a proofreader; I can spot typos a mile awya!
5. I have a very keen eye and notice when a single electron is out of place; I'm the only person I know who can *see* static electricity.

A "true" to number 1 is normal, but if you answered "true" to number 2 *too,* you really should get to know your spouse better! Put this book down and go away for the weekend! A "true" to number 3 is a good start. Still, error isn't quite the focus here; rather, we're going to exercise something more subtle. And a "true" to number 4? Say, you wouldn't like to apply for a job as my assistant, would you? "True" to number 5? You're lucky if you still *have* a spouse!

The exercises throughout this half of the chapter will relate to some of the greatest artists of the Renaissance, that period when the flowering of Western civilization served as a bridge from the Middle Ages to modern times.

The Middle Ages (the first few centuries of which have been termed the "Dark Ages") began with the fall of Rome around the fifth century A.D. and lasted until the fourteenth century, when the Renaissance began to emerge in Italy. Long periods of repression typically end with a burst of creativity, and perhaps there is no better example than the Renaissance. Elsewhere in Europe, we may date the Renaissance from the fifteenth century to the seventeenth century, but throughout the Western world, there is no doubt that this was one of the grandest ages of humankind. Culturally, it was a time of brilliant accomplishment in all sorts of scholarship, including science, literature, and the arts. New value was given to worldly experience and to the dignity of man. While much of the unique beauty of antiquity was lost forever through the subsequent "dark" centuries, in the Renaissance it was slowly replaced with a burgeoning of intellect and new beauty.

In the Middle Ages, artists had been respected, but they had been considered little more than craftsmen, like blacksmiths or carpenters. With the advent of the Renaissance, however, artists began to become exalted figures—supermen, in a way. In the following exercises, you'll see a very famous and/or important work painted by a Renaissance master. Study it briefly, but thoughtfully. Afterward, you'll see it again, but this time something will be wrong with it. Without looking back at the original, try to determine what the change is.

JAN VAN EYCK (Flemish, c. 1390–1441) was one of the first artists to capture the intense observation of the action of light and how it could be used to define form, shape, and texture, as well as convey mood. The clarity and realism of his paintings were so vivid that many painters attempted to imitate his style and failed, causing a reaction against it— perhaps the ultimate expression of envy.

The Arnolfi Wedding
NATIONAL GALLERY, LONDON

The Arnolfi Wedding is an illustration of the transition from the medieval world to that of the Renaissance. While both realistic and meticulous, it has been seen as symbolic, although interpretations of those symbols vary. For example, why is a dog present? (Is it a symbol of loyalty—in this case, marital fidelity?) Try to find the error below.

1. Not *The Arnolfi Wedding*

HIERONYMOUS BOSCH (Flemish, c. 1450–1516) was one of the last painters who reflected the medieval sensibility, favoring satire, pessimism, and the mundane. Though the imagery of his works seems strange, surreal, and in dire need of explanation, his contemporaries would have known and understood these images, as they were culled from symbols familiar to them.

Garden of Delights

PRADO, MADRID

Garden of Delights is actually a triptych—a painting divided into three panels—and the portion called "Hell" is depicted here. This is an example of an extremist tendency to depict the bizarre and the weird, unusual for these early Renaissance years, and very jarring. Can you find the error below? (Good luck.)

2. Not
Garden of Delights

GIOTTO DI BORDONE (Italian, c. 1266–1337) was one of the earliest true Renaissance painters, who, as a group, returned to the artistic sensibilities of ancient times. Leaving two-dimensional Byzantine art completely behind, he perfected depth in his paintings and imparted emotion not seen in hundreds of years.

The Lamentation
SCROVEGNI CHAPEL, PADUA

The Lamentation is a fresco—a painting done on fresh, moist plaster—
and depicts mourners grieving over the dead body of Christ. An example
of an entirely new style of painting, it rejects Byzantine flatness, instead
rendering characters in a shallow setting, blocked as if they were in a
scene from a movie or a stage play. Do you see the error below?

3. Not *The Lamentation*

MASACCIO (nickname of Tommaso di Giovanni) (Italian, 1401–1428?) was the first to use settings with the one-point perspective system, which brought the observer closer to the painting and made him a part of it, so to speak. In only six years Masaccio brought about a revolution in the art world, before leaving for Rome in his mid-20's, never to be heard from again.

The Holy Trinity
SANTA MARIA NOVELLA,
FLORENCE

The Holy Trinity has been called one of the first true Renaissance paintings. Not only does it exhibit the quiet power and simple dignity of ancient Greek and Roman art, its figures are carefully placed within an architectural setting that is geometrically accurate in perspective. What error can you find below?

4. Not
*The Holy
Trinity*

SANDRO BOTTICELLI (né Alessandro di Mariano Filipepi) (Italian, c. 1445—1510) created a series of serene paintings based on ancient myths. In fact, however, he had a very unusual temperament and the serenity of his paintings was usually the request of the patrons who commissioned them. He was less restrained when left to his own devices. He eventually joined a religious crusade that reacted against the "vanities" of the Renaissance in Florence.

The Birth of Venus
UFFIZI MUSEUM, FLORENCE

The Birth of Venus demonstrates Botticelli's concern with the movement of figures on the canvas, as suggested by an outstretched arm, flowing hair, or a billowing cape. New studies of the depiction of human anatomy lent a greater sense of realism to works such as this, but a more decorative style was adopted as well. Do you see the error below?

5. Not The Birth of Venus

Here's what was wrong with those masterpieces. For the most part, instead of simply introducing a random error, an error was created that defied the description you read. For example, when we mentioned that an artist was an expert in perspective, we enlarged a figure out of proper proportion. These were the specific changes:

1. Not *The Arnolfi Wedding*—The dog has become a cat.
2. Not *Garden of Delights*—As strange as "Hell" was, not even it could have portrayed Napoleon, who wasn't yet born.
3. Not *The Lamentation*—A mourner has been added, who is distant from the shallow stage setting for the characters.
4. Not *The Holy Trinity*—The figure of Christ has been enlarged out of proper proportion.
5. Not *The Birth of Venus*—The hair of the main character is no longer fluttering and even appears to be tightly held.

What's Wrong?

How did you do? As you see now, the point here was not to find silly errors, but rather to learn how to size up a situation and pay attention, a skill that we shouldn't leave back in our locker at college along with our old gym shoes. For example, this is one of the ways a physician starts on the path to a diagnosis. If there's anything to see, he or she may be sizing up a problem the moment you walk through the door.

Paying attention, even without knowing it, can make the difference between life and death. I was once crossing a busy New York street with my daughter and suddenly had the impulse to run, which we did—just seconds before three cars collided directly behind us, right where we'd been crossing, sending bits of glass and pieces of twisted metal flying. My daughter's head had been turned toward me at the time, but as I was looking in the other direction, I had happened to see subtle signs of an impending accident, signs that I no longer remember clearly: hands turning a steering wheel too quickly, a fleeting look of alarm on the face of a passing motorist, an unexpected movement in an ominous direction.

We hope, of course, that you won't be called upon to avoid death routinely and that you don't often find yourself in a police officer's uniform walking down an alley that suddenly becomes just a little too quiet.

But even so, paying attention is a skill worth cultivating. If you're like me, you can pick up the morning paper and zero right in on the typo on the front page with laserlike vision. Then you arrive at work, type an interoffice memo, proofread it, and drop a message on the desk of your neighbor's office that reads, "Sorry I can't make it for lunch today, after all. I'm going to be in a meeting late. But how about later this geek?"

Why? Sheer carelessness? Not really. Don't be too hard on yourself. (Or on us!) Rather, the point is that if we have too relaxed an intellectual attitude, we'll have a tendency to create familiar patterns where they don't exist. We'll see what we expect to see— or worse, what we simply *want* to see. And wishful thinking is the bane of the strong intellect.

Here's a little help in finding the errors to come in the rest of the chapter. First, remember that we'll create "errors" that aren't necessarily wrong in themselves, *but that contradict the text.* That's the sort of observation, both visual and mental, that will help you in everyday life. There's nothing really "wrong" with a circuit-breaker switch that has flipped to the other side, but noticing it can tell you why your microwave oven doesn't work. There are plenty of things in life that behave much like that circuit-breaker switch, and we could benefit greatly if only we paid more attention to them.

And because we'll be contradicting the text, the "errors" will be significant ones. However, don't mistake "large" for "significant" or vice versa—which applies to life, as well. Nor should you pay more attention to intriguing objects than to prosaic ones, which is how the magician so readily fools us. He or she distracts with one hand while concealing with the other. So often and in so many ways, we turn to the object of apparent interest instead of the object of most importance.

Consider Sherlock Holmes and his keen eye. Attention to detail, both great and small, enabled him to make many of his cognitive leaps. We all have this ability, even if we don't exercise it. Why not start paying a little more attention in life? The next time you see street-dancers, stop and watch. But not the performance. Instead, stand some distance back from the crowd and watch how the pickpockets operate.

LEONARDO DA VINCI (Italian, 1459–1519) was a true "Renaissance man" and explored many fields in his desire for mastery of the canvas. He became interested in things like the movement of water, the flight of birds, and human anatomy, and because he was a skilled draftsman, he was able to depict not only those, but the workings of mechanical objects, as well.

Mona Lisa
LOUVRE, PARIS

The *Mona Lisa* may be the most famous painting in the world, judging from the awesome number of tourists jostling each other to get a look at the famous smile and sidelong glance of it in the Louvre museum in Paris, bypassing an awesome number of beautiful works of art to do so. The question is, "Why?" I don't know. But even though the painting was never finished, it revolutionized portrait painting.

6. Not *Mona Lisa*

MICHELANGELO BUONARROTI (Italian, 1475–1546) was the other giant of the High Renaissance. Although he considered himself first and foremost a sculptor, he is probably best known for the painting of the ceiling of the Sistine Chapel, which was recognized as an unparalleled masterpiece in its own time and earned the artist the title of "the divine Michelangelo."

The Creation of Adam
VATICAN CITY, SISTINE CHAPEL, ROME

The *Creation of Adam*, with its significant space between the hand of Adam and the hand of God, is the most famous of all the sections on the ceiling of the Sistine Chapel, which also includes eight other scenes from the Creation. The artist dismissed his assistants and executed the entire project alone, which took him more than four years. Do you see the error?

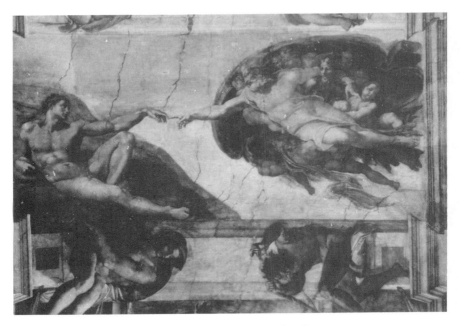

7. Not *The Creation of Adam*

TITIAN (Tiziano Vecellino) (Italian, c. 1477–1576), whose stature grew to be at least as great as Michelangelo's, was recognized as having been to Venice what Leonardo was to Florence. One of the longest-lived of the Renaissance painters, he also possessed one of the widest ranges in subject matter, painting everything from portraits to mythological figures, and from madonnas to the profane.

Rape of Europa

ISABELLA STEWART GARDNER MUSEUM, BOSTON

Rape of Europa demonstrates the artist's command of grand form and action in his later years, when he strove for increased dramatic and emotional content in his images. (By the way, "rape" as used in classical mythology and art history refers largely to "abduction," so don't be misled.) Color is applied with a free hand. Do you see the error below?

8. Not *Rape of Europa*

RAPHAEL (Raffaello Sanzio) (Italian, 1483–1520), one of the three masters of the High Renaissance (in addition to Leonardo and Michelangelo), could also be considered its child prodigy; his great talent was acknowledged well before he was twenty years old. Although Raphael probably was not the most exciting or brilliant of the masters, he seemed never to make a mistake and came the closest of the three to turning painting into a science.

The School of Athens
ST. PETER'S BASILICA, VATICAN CITY, ROME

The School of Athens is one of the best examples of the High Renaissance style. The artist casts his characters in a bountiful variety of poses, yet manages to weave them and their gestures together in such a way as to present a unified pattern that leads to the cardinal figures of Plato and Aristotle at the converging point of the perspective. Can you find the error?

9. Not *The School of Athens*

ALBRECHT DÜRER (German, 1471–1528) may have been one of the first non-Italian artists to understand and utilize the great strides the Italians had made, having spent considerable time in Italy studying painting while the art was being revolutionized by da Vinci and others. Dürer's early work as an engraver and woodcutter made him widely known, second only to the Italians.

Four Apostles

ALTE PINAKOTHEK, MUNICH

The *Four Apostles* is an example of the combination of the heroic images of the Italian High Renaissance and German art's traditional passion for complexity and attention to detail. The artist's admiration for Venetian artists in particular is shown in the quality of light and the folds of the draperies. But there's an error below, as usual. Do you know what it is?

10. Not the *Four Apostles*

And here's what was wrong with those masterpieces:

6. Not The *Mona Lisa*—Here her gaze is directed more forward. She's less enigmatic when she's looking directly at you, isn't she?
7. Not The *Creation of Adam*—The extended fingers are now actually touching.
8. Not *Rape of Europe*—The dramatic and vibrant sky is now flat and dull.
9. Not *The School of Athens*—The eye of the observer is now led over the heads of the two central figures.
10. Not *Four Apostles*—Their clothes need ironing!

How did you do this time? If you felt that you did quite a bit better, it's probably because you knew ahead of time that learning the text would help prepare you for the coming error. Knowledge (which you had for the first five artists) wasn't good enough without attention, and attention (which you gave to the first five flawed paintings) wasn't good enough without knowledge.

The more knowledge you have, the better, of course. But no one can be an expert in everything, and mastery of even one area is very difficult to attain. Instead of depending on a knowledge base, then, we need to learn to pay attention in general. But how?

In general, we need to steer clear of habit. Let's use travel as an example. Some people have become so habituated to their surroundings, so used to their hometown, that they feel completely overwhelmed by anything strange or foreign, sometimes going so far as to never even leave their "home" state.

"Oh, I just don't *like* to travel," someone might say. "I like it here just fine." But what that person likes isn't necessarily their own little corner of the world, wherever that may happen to be. They like the familiarity. And that doesn't sufficiently justify not traveling. After all, people can have that fabulous familiarity fifty out of fifty-two weeks a year and still take vacations out of town, can't they? No, they don't like to travel because they've become so helpless around the unfamiliar.

That's how habit can stunt intellectual growth, and we've all seen real-life cases. The kid who is never allowed to leave his own backyard is hopelessly inept in a public playground; the young woman who becomes enamored of bridge eventually begins to have difficulty reading a book; the old man who makes himself a sandwich for dinner every evening can't handle the prospect of being given a basket full of fresh vegetables and a plump chicken. Life becomes an obstacle course instead of a richly varied experience.

Variety is not only the proverbial "spice of life"—it is also essential to broader intellectual competence. If you like to play games, don't play just one or two; constantly try new ones. Whenever you're "on the road," don't use the same one or two hotel chains; stay in a different place each night. The same goes for chain restaurants; try a different "mom and pop" place every day. Choosing the familiar may be easier in the short run, but in the long run, it's like choosing not to exercise.

Picture Completion
What's Missing?

Do you notice when "something's missing?"

1.
2. I seldom seem to notice that something is missing until I need it.
3. I'll be walking peacefully out to the parking lot after a shopping trip, when I'll notice, with a sudden start and for no reason at all, that I've left something behind.
4. Sometimes I'll close the front door behind me, stop in my tracks, and say to myself, "Wait a minute. I feel like I'm missing something."
5. When I'm in a restaurant, I'll often say, "It's not that this doesn't taste good. It just seems like something's missing."

Number 1? Sorry, we just couldn't resist. "True" to number 2? Maybe you're a little inattentive. "True" to number 3? Not so bad. You forget something, but notice it missing before long. A "true" to number 4 shows attentiveness, not an obsessive/compulsive nature (unless you go back inside repeatedly to make sure you turned things off/on/down/up). And a "true" to number 5? I do it myself. Usually what's missing is simply a good cook.

Let's begin with some exercises (no, no, *they're* not going to be "what's missing" in this section!), all of which pertain to great artists who emerged *after* the Renaissance. Unfortunately, there's no way to condense this time span without truly significant omissions, so let us just mention here that these are only a few of the highlights.

"Baroque" (early—seventeenth to mid—eighteenth centuries) was a style of painting typified by elaborate ornamentation and a good deal of symmetry, and enhanced by the high-contrast effects of strong chiaroscuro—the technique of using light and dark for dramatic effect. Deep perspective was developed, and color was exploited to its maximum. "Baroque" yielded gradually to "rococo" (early to mid—eighteenth century), which was at once similar, yet in a way almost opposite. Elegance remained a feature of painting, but the colors softened, the curves became more delicate, and the activities depicted grew quieter, lending a certain overall charming effect to the scenes.

After that, "neoclassicism" (mid—eighteenth to mid—nineteenth centuries) became fashionable, returning the canvas to classical aesthetics and forms, complete with Greek and Roman heroes, relatively realistic images, and a concern with political subjects. "Romantic" art (late—eighteenth to late—nineteenth centuries) expressed the emotional and irrational side of humankind, in high contrast to the idealism of the neoclassicists. "Realism" (mid to late—nineteenth century) subsequently arose out of a desire to paint what was actually there—not heroes, but ordinary people and those living in poverty on the streets.

CARAVAGGIO (né Michelangelo Merisi) (Italian, 1573–1610) was instrumental in founding a type of baroque painting called "naturalism," which was concerned with the accurate representation of nature. In fact, Caravaggio's religious scenes were painted with such unflattering accuracy that his patrons often refused to pay him or else had the paintings retouched.

Supper at Emmaus
NATIONAL GALLERY, LONDON

Supper at Emmaus features a soft, almost overweight, and clean-shaven Christ, and although the artist was known as a true innovator, this sort of "naturalism" caused him no end of trouble. One altarpiece he painted was denounced as vulgar and even sacrilegious, and the clergy forced him to do another one. What's missing below?

1. Not *Supper at Emmaus*

PETER PAUL RUBENS (Flemish, 1577–1640) was the archetypal baroque artist. His occupation as a diplomat took him to many foreign lands, and he came into contact with numerous artists and styles. Eventually, his studio became an artistic center for leading painters and patrons in Europe, creating a virtual art industry, which turned out paintings for churches, royals, and other nobles.

Rape of the Daughters of Leucippus
ALTE PINAKOTHEK, MUNICH

Rape of the Daughters of Leucippus illustrates one of the artist's most famous strengths, one which modern critics seem to dislike the most: his skill at depicting the sensuality of human flesh. If you're still a bit Victorian, that disturbs you, but if you're not, it's one of the things that draws you to Rubens. What's missing below?

2. Not Rape of the Daughters of Leucippus

Diego Rodríguez de Silva y VELÁZQUEZ (Spanish, 1599—1660) is probably best known for his portraits of royalty, but he was just as able to infuse a portrayal of a court jester with dignity. Much of the attention of Velázquez was focused on human tragedy; to him, the poor, the suffering, and the handicapped were of as much interest as a king.

King Philip IV
PRADO, MADRID

King Philip IV illustrates a quality of the artist's early work—a concern for everyday reality, such as the folded piece of paper the monarch is holding. At times, seemingly insignificant objects become just as important as the human figures, and some of the works of Velázquez elevate the picayune to the eternal. Can you tell what's missing below?

3. Not *King Philip IV*

REMBRANDT VAN RIJN (Dutch, 1606–69), probably the most famous artist in the world, even if not the best, was among the first to prove that the handling of paint, light, and color could be as important as the actual subject of the work. Upon his death, he left over six hundred paintings, a hundred of them self-portraits, the images forming a striking series of the great man aging.

The Night Watch
RIJKSMUSEUM, AMSTERDAM

Sortie of the Shooting Company of Captain Frans Banning Cocq was once believed to depict a night scene because of an old revarnishing and the accumulation of dirt, hence its popular name *The Night Watch*; it wasn't properly cleaned until 1947. Later Rembrandt portraits are notable for the use of light to reveal character. Notice anything missing below?

4. Not *The Night Watch*

JAN VERMEER (Joannes van der Meer) (Dutch, 1632–75) was better known to his contemporaries as an art dealer than a painter, but it is unclear whether he was ever able to sell any of his own paintings. More than half of those attributed to him were found in his own house and studio, and he died in poverty.

The Love Letter

RIJKSMUSEUM, AMSTERDAM

The Love Letter is considered by many people to be the finest example of how Vermeer achieved the "you are there" intimacy in his interior paintings. He extended the immediate foreground into the observer's own space, setting a portion of a table or chair there, as if the observer were actually standing by it. Anything missing below?

5. Not *The Love Letter*

Here's what was missing from those masterpieces. Again, for the most part, instead of simply removing any object at random, one was removed that contradicted the description you read:

1. Not *Supper at Emmaus*—The supper is missing.
2. Not *Rape of the Daughters of Leucippus*—The textured skin tones have been removed.
3. Not *King Philip IV*—The piece of paper is gone.
4. Not *The Night Watch*—One of the main subjects is missing.
5. Not *The Love Letter*—The foreground objects have been removed.

What's Missing?

How did you do? (And aren't you glad we didn't pick Duchamp's *Nude Descending a Staircase,* which has no nude and no staircase to begin with?) If you did better than in the first half of the chapter, your attentiveness is improving considerably. It's usually much more difficult to notice an omission than it is to notice an object that doesn't belong there. If you looked out the window of a New York City skyscraper and studied the skyline for a few moments, you'd probably notice if an apartment building in the distance was on fire or had been painted lavender, but would you notice if it weren't there? Even if you were very familiar with the view? (I'm doing this right now, and I do happen to see one fire. But that's because it's a quiet day in Manhattan.)

Think about the view from your own window, either at the office or at home. Can you picture the scene clearly in your mind's eye? And we don't mean a vague blur of buildings or trees. We mean a clear picture, the sort you could use to actually count the windows on the buildings or the branches on the trees. You can't, of course. And that's normal.

As we mentioned earlier, the mind may see what it "wants" to see (including what it is "used" to seeing), regardless of whether something is added, something is wrong, or something is missing. How many times have you searched everywhere for your favorite ballpoint pen only to find it in your pencil cup? How many times have you searched everywhere for the television's remote control only to find it lying on top of the set? Or worse, in your hand?

There are quite a few ways to sharpen your performance on a "What's Missing?" test. Here are a few:

(1) Think about the significance. The missing element will probably be important; even if small, it will still be a major detail. (2) Think about form. It's harder to notice missing elements that don't disturb the symmetry, so look at the center alone, but look at both sides as a pair. Consider a cartoon character. If it has no nose, you probably won't notice that. Likewise, if both ears are missing, you won't notice that, either. But if only *one* ear is missing, you'll see that immediately. (3) Think about function. If an object is as pictured, will it operate? Doors must have knobs; lamps must have cords. (4) Check for corresponding elements. If there's a sun, there may be shadows. If there's a mirror, there may be a reflection.

JEAN-ANTOINE WATTEAU (French, 1684–1721), along with Boucher and Fragonard, was one of the top three rococo artists. He created paintings known as *fêtes galantes,* wistful fantasies with an elegant quality. Later rococo artists infused their work with a strongly erotic content, and although refined throughout, much of it is criticized today for having little underlying meaning.

Embarkation for Cythera
LOUVRE, PARIS

Embarkation for Cythera is a true *fête galante*—having sensitive characterizations, delicacy of color and technique, and an idyllic setting. Watteau's world was the fantasy world of the fairy tale, a world where men and women were gods and goddesses; his patrons were the wealthiest of Frenchmen, who found heaven on earth in his works. What's missing here?

6. Not *Embarkation for Cythera*

JACQUES-LOUIS DAVID (French, 1748–1825) was the leader of the neo-classical movement, a revival of the spirit of antiquity. Although David was trained in the rococo tradition, he rebelled against the frivolous, although visually pleasing images of the recent past and advocated a return to the severe, yet simple style of the Roman era.

Oath of the Horatii
LOUVRE, PARIS

Oath of the Horatii made such a strong political statement that guards were posted to protect it when it was first shown in Paris. The painting was recognized immediately as a seminal work; the subject matter itself was a call to arms—both artistically and politically—advocating a return to the more austere, ancient values of the early Roman republic. What's missing?

7. Not *Oath of the Horatii*

FRANCISCO JOSÉ DE GOYA y Lucientes (Spanish, 1746–1828) was probably the greatest painter of the new romantic period. Less a style than
an attitude, "romanticism" does not refer to "love"; rather, it stresses the
whole range of human emotion, the loveliness of nature, and the intrigue
of the exotic or mysterious. After an illness left him deaf, Goya's work
became even more intense.

The Third of May (Executions)
PRADO, MADRID

The Third of May (Executions) illustrates that romanticism has less to do with romantic love than it does with passion. This painting is a frightening portrayal of the horrors of war and a powerful indictment of the French during the Napoleonic Wars in Spain; a "sister" painting, not depicted here, is called *The Second of May (Uprising)*. What's missing?

8. Not *The Third of May (Executions)*

(Ferdinand Victor) EUGÈNE DELACROIX (French, 1798–1863) was the leading French romantic painter of his time. He studied extensively in order to perfect his art, making use of nascent photography to explore forms, as well as investigating the science of color values. He chose figures from great literature for subjects, while transmuting current events into greater historical perspective for the canvas.

Liberty Leading the People
LOUVRE, PARIS

Liberty Leading the People depicts the action and excitement of the French Revolution of 1830, showing men of different classes battling at the gates of Paris. With such politically inspired works as well as with others, the artist's emotional intensity frequently proved disturbing to the respectability and complacency of the salons. Do you notice anything conspicuously absent below?

9. Not *Liberty Leading the People*

(Jean-Désiré-) GUSTAVE COURBET (French, 1819–77) was highly controversial for his arrogance and his open contempt for the Church and other authorities. To many of us, the term "realism" refers to visual accuracy; however, in painting it refers more to a portrayal of the more ordinary activities of everyday life. His works were considered especially offensive in this regard and aroused savage criticism.

The Stone Breakers
GEMÄLDEGALERIE, DRESDEN

The Stone Breakers was destroyed during World War II, but it remains one of Courbet's most famous paintings. The artist's depiction of the common man showed great personal concern for the poor, and no matter how lowly was the subject of his work, he always gave him or her a great dignity without succumbing to naive idealization. What's missing below?

10. Not *The Stone Breakers*

For the last time, here's what's missing from those masterpieces:

6. Not *Embarkation for Cythera*—The sky is now flat and uninteresting.
7. Not *Oath of the Horatii*—The symbolic swords are now gone.
8. Not *The Third of May (Executions)*—The firing squad's weapons are absent.
9. Not *Liberty Leading the People*—Liberty has lost her flag, making her appear as though she leads the people with a raised fist.
10. Not *The Stone Breakers*—The stubborn stones themselves have disappeared.

How did you do this time? Maybe you did quite a bit better, and if you did, congratulations. You're becoming more alert, and that's really the skill we're exercising here. The point behind "What's wrong?" and "What's missing?" is alertness to our surroundings, and we addressed that point by focusing it on great works of art.

In order to find "what's missing," we must first determine that something *is* missing, and this skill is more important than is commonly realized. The intellectual understanding that something *is* missing can underlie everything from the arts to the sciences. Here's just one well-known example, of which there are surely many.

One of the most aggressive anthropological endeavors over the past century has been the search for the "missing link," that theoretical primate (or primates) postulated to close the gap in the evolutionary chain between the anthropoid apes and man. And how did that hypothesis arise? Have a look at primitive man. He's ugly, unkempt, hairy, and barely civilized. (But you could say the same of many college fraternity members!) That is, he is still very recognizably human. Then have a look at the anthropoid apes. There are many strikingly similar characteristics, but you're never going to mistake one for the other. (Although this can depend on what kind of friends you have!)

Evolutionists looked at these two groups and said, "Hmm. If evolution is correct, and we emerged along these lines, something must be missing. The gap is just too great." (Of course, they didn't investigate *all* the fraternities!) And so they proposed the idea of a "missing link"—a creature with both primate characteristics and human ones.

But it's not necessary to be a scientist to benefit from the skills that enable us to cope with errors and omissions. Strengthening these abilities helps empower us in nearly every area of thinking and in subjects ranging from top-flight critical analysis to social skills. "What's wrong?" and "What's missing?" are questions asked by the five-star general, by the efficiency expert, by the social worker, and by the parent alike.

BOOK TEN

Similarities and Differences

Apparent

How easily can you spot the similar aspects of concepts you normally assume to be very different?

1. I can't compare "apples" and "oranges."
2. They say no two snowflakes are alike, and I think that's true. I've seen plenty close up, and no two were the same.
3. I like to think that there is no one else like me in the world and that I'm unique.
4. At first, people seem very different—different skin color, religious beliefs, or sexual orientation—but when I know more about them personally, I realize they're not all that different.
5. I can *always* find a common ground or a common goal; what I'd really like to be is a diplomat in Bosnia.

A "true" to number 1 is normal because we've heard the phrase so often, but we *can* compare apples and oranges. "True" to number 2 and even number 3 is normal, although both statements are flawed for the same reason; while our unique qualities should not be undervalued, we have far more in common with other people than we have differences. "True" to number 4? That's realistic. And "true" to number 5?! Maybe that's not!

These exercises provide a brief overview of world religions:

Here are the three main divisions of Christianity—the religion based on the worship of Jesus Christ in the Trinity of God the Father, the Son, and the Holy Spirit, and on the Old and New Testaments of the Bible, the latter of which offers information about Christ's birth, life, and death.

ROMAN CATHOLICISM organizes its church under a government of bishops; although each church largely governs itself, each one acknowledges the supreme authority of the Pope in Rome. The rites of salvation are enacted through the Eucharist, or Mass, and other sacraments—such as baptism, confirmation, matrimony, penance (confession and contrition), anointing of the ill, and holy orders (making a man capable of performing the Eucharist) and through the Divine Office, the public prayer of the Church.

PROTESTANTISM began with the Reformation and emphasizes the authority of the Bible. The Reformers protested that the Roman Catholics had erred in allowing the Church itself, and especially the Pope, to take a place of authority equal to the written word. However, as most scholars do not find any particular church government taught by the Scriptures, Protestants are free to develop the forms that they themselves feel is best for the propagation of the Gospel; the clergy is set apart only for organizational purposes, and the priesthood is for all believers. All Protestants agree in reducing the seven sacraments of Roman Catholics to two: baptism and the Lord's Supper.

EASTERN ORTHODOXY is a family of self-governing Christian churches that share the same faith and follow the same laws. However, they are not connected to the Roman Catholic or Protestant churches, having separated from Rome before the Reformation because of the insertion of "and the Son" directly after "from the Father" in liturgical texts; the change was deeply offensive to the Eastern Church. The Reformation retained the phrase, though, so Protestants agree with Roman Catholics on this point. Moreover, the Eastern Patriarch is not an Eastern pope, but merely the first in honor among equals.

Here are some questions:

1. Name two apparent similarities shared by the three Christian religions.
2. Without repeating what you said above, name one apparent similarity shared by Protestantism and Eastern Orthodoxy.

Here are the four contemporary branches of Judaism, the religion that believes that God, speaking through Moses at Sinai, gave instructions to the Children of Israel in rules that must be obeyed. The Revelation at Sinai, recorded in the five books of Moses (commonly known as the Torah) is the basis of all Jewish law, including the law that states that only the children (and all the children) who are born to Jewish women can call themselves Jews.

ORTHODOX JUDAISM upholds the ethical and practical imperatives of traditional Judaism, including the importance of the Sabbath, the rabbi, and the strict dietary laws.

REFORM JUDAISM resulted from an effort to modernize Orthodox Judaism, leading to a rejection of the strictest of the laws, such as the dietary ones and the ones requiring head-covering. It also asserted that any land of Jewish residence was home.

CONSERVATIVE JUDAISM resulted from a partial rejection of Reform Judaism. It reaffirmed the importance of Jewish nationhood, the Land of Israel, and the Hebrew language. Conservative Jews observe the moral rules of traditional Judaism.

HASIDIC JUDAISM is a mystical movement founded in the eighteenth century. Hasidic Jews believe the soul is rooted in a Divine Being, and through self-denial, devotion, and trust in rabbis who work miracles, they can attain a closer relationship to God.

And here are some questions:

3. Name two apparent similarities shared by Orthodox, Reform, Conservative, and Hasidic Jews.
4. Without repeating what you said above, name one apparent similarity shared by Reform and Conservative Judaism.

Another important monotheistic religion is Islam, which means "submission," the role that Muslims believe describes the appropriate relationship between man and God (Allah). The sacred book of Islam is the *Koran,* composed of revelations that came to Mohammed after his call to prophethood, and the duties of Muslims to God are known as the Five Pillars of Islam.

SUNNAH signifies "the example set by the Prophet" and generally means the traditional way. However, issues raised by early factions caused the Sunni Muslims to define their own doctrinal positions in turn. Their world view states that nothing exists except God, whose being is the only real being.

SHIA originated in controversies that followed the death of Mohammed, and there are several disparate Shiite sects, all of which emphasize idealism and transcendentalism. The violent death of Ali's (son-in-law of the Prophet) son is marked with passion plays and emotional frenzy, sometimes even self-mutilation.

And here's one more question:

5. Name one apparent similarity shared by Sunni and Shiite Muslims.

Although there are no absolute answers to the questions above, here are a few samples: (1) They all believe in the Trinity, and they all use the Old and New Testaments of the Bible as Scripture, (2) They both broke with the Roman Catholic Church and/or neither of them have a pope as a supreme authority, (3) They all believe in the same God, and they all use the books of Moses as the basis for their laws and ethics, (4) They are both less strict than Orthodox Judaism, and (5) They both believe that Mohammed is the Prophet of God and/or they both use the *Koran* as the basis for their laws and ethics and/or they both abide by the Five Pillars of Islam.

If you belong to any of these faiths, you might find it interesting to study some of the others, especially the ones most similar to your own. It might surprise you to discover that "neighboring" faiths are not as different as you may think.

Apparent Similarities

Understanding similarities can be a great help in solving problems, both on tests and in real life, of course. An inability to transfer knowledge from one task to another would leave a television repairman completely incapable of servicing anything but the brands he'd studied in school, and it would leave a general incapable of orchestrating an armed conflict anywhere but at home. And speaking of armed conflict at home, understanding similarities can even help people avoid problems in choosing another marriage partner after a divorce—unless James Boswell is correct in his terming a second marriage (after an unhappy one) "the triumph of hope over experience."

Think about what it was like back in school when you had to solve problems on a test that were similar (or could be solved in a similar manner) to examples the instructor had illustrated in class. The problems may have used different terms, and they may have been disguised, but if you were able to relate to the similarities between them and the ones you knew, you were able to solve the problem (unless you'd missed class on the fateful day, an experience we all share).

In fact, the bulk of human knowledge has relied heavily on finding similarities among seemingly different things. Now-known laws of biology resulted, in part, from scientists who could see the connection between, say, a crustacean and a human being. Among the similarities: both have organs that perform functions in common, both need to eat, both have sexual urges, and both desire occasionally to grab someone's nose with large pincers.

How do we learn to develop this ability to find similarities in life? Practice. And it's easy. Just take any subject—politics is always good for endless discussion—and discuss with friends the similarities between your views and theirs. Best of all, make friends with people who have apparently opposing views and look for ways in which their opinions converge. (And even if you don't find any significant similarity, you'll at least have made a new friend and learned something. You may even decide—heaven forbid— that you should change your mind.)

Or you can even make a game of it with the kids. But don't be surprised if you lose often; kids have a way of zeroing in on things that your education has taught you to glide over. As you're sitting in a waiting room, relaxing on a train ride, or driving a car, one person chooses (quickly) any two disparate objects at random (say, a snail and an Amtrak train—no, that's too easy—make that a traffic light and a street sign), and the other person replies with one way in which they're similar. The first person then replies with another way, and the two of you reply back and forth until one of you is completely stuck. Then if the other can name just one more mutually acceptable similarity, he or she wins. (Alternate choosing each time.)

This sort of thing can be fun. My assistant once wrote a paper comparing (and contrasting, I hope) *Oedipus Rex* to an episode of "The Brady Bunch." Yes, it drew laughter, but it also drew an A. (But would you believe he was in the *sixteenth* grade at the time?)

Back to more exercises.

As one of the largest religions in the world, it's not surprising that Christianity has taken many forms; the majority of them are Protestant. Here are the three "classical" Protestant denominations:

LUTHERANS follow the example set by Martin Luther, who complained about corruption among the clergy and advocated worship in national languages instead of Latin. He also favored a married clergy rather than a celibate one. (Contrary to common belief, "celibate" originally meant simply "unmarried.")

REFORMED CHURCHES, including the Presbyterians, consider themselves to be the Roman Catholic Church, but reformed by John Calvin, among others. They took the Lutheran principle "by faith alone" and added "to God alone the glory," emphasizing that God's word alone should establish the basis for faith.

ANGLICAN COMMUNION, including the Episcopal Church, arises from the Church of England and has few written rules. United under the Archbishop of Canterbury as its leader, its practices are defined in the *Book of Common Prayer*. During the Reformation, the Church broke with the Pope, but not with the Catholic Faith.

Here are some questions:

6. Name two apparent similarities shared by the Lutheran, Reformed, and Anglican Communion churches.
7. Name one apparent similarity shared by the Reformed and Anglican Communion churches.

Here are some other Protestant denominations that have appeared since the Reformation:

BAPTISTS share the basic beliefs of most Protestants, but some stress that they have no human founder, no human authority, and no human creed. They also feel strongly that only believers should be baptized and that this must be accomplished by immersion rather than by the symbolic sprinkling of water.

METHODISTS are highly institutionalized and emphasize the teaching of Christian perfection along with an insistence on the personal aspects of religion and its social application. Their allegiance is to doctrines of the historic creeds, and they rely upon the *Book of Common Prayer* for guidance.

PENTECOSTALISM is a diverse style of belief that includes miracles, supernatural healing, spirit possession, speaking in tongues, and exorcism. Although this is most common among non-Christians, Pentecostals believe in Christian doctrines and also in Fundamentalism, a literal interpretation of the Bible.

DISCIPLES OF CHRIST comprise three main bodies: The Churches of Christ (Disciples of Christ) practice a dynamic evangelism based on a literal interpretation of the Bible. The Christian Church (Disciples of Christ) has developed a strong missionary involvement. The Undenominational Fellowship of Christian Churches and Churches of Christ were identified with the Disciples but refused to follow them into the Christian Church; they practice a relatively uncomplicated biblical faith.

Here are some more questions:

8. Name two apparent similarities shared by the Baptists, the Methodists, the Pentecostals, and the Disciples of Christ.
9. Name one apparent similarity shared by the Pentecostals and the Disciples of Christ.

And here are three non-Protestant Christian religions that have appeared since the Reformation:

The CHURCH OF JESUS CHRIST OF LATTER DAY SAINTS, also known as the Mormon Church, did not arise from any other group. It was founded by Joseph Smith in the early nineteenth century. Mormons believe in early Christian doctrines and that life is spent in surmounting obstacles and increasing faith in order eventually to achieve perfection and become gods themselves in an afterlife.

JEHOVAH'S WITNESSES consider their founder to be Jehovah and teach that Jesus Christ is his son, but the modern church was established by Charles Taze Russell in the late nineteenth century. Their beliefs are based strictly on the Bible, and they forecast an eventual Armageddon to rid the world of evil. All Witnesses are ministers and many make house-to-house visits.

CHURCH OF CHRIST, SCIENTIST was organized by a woman named Mary Baker Eddy in the late nineteenth century. Although the Church's name includes the word "scientist," Christian Scientists do not use modern medicine outside of childbirth; instead, they believe that the experience of true spiritual reality is the ultimate scientific fact.

And here is one last question:

10. Name one apparent similarity shared by Mormons, Jehovah's Witnesses, and Christian Scientists.

Again, there are no absolute answers, but here are a few samples: (6) They are all "classical" Protestant denominations, and they are all directly descended from denominations that broke with Rome, (7) Both consider themselves to be the Catholic Church without the supreme authority of a pope, (8) All consider themselves to be Christian, but without the Catholic Church, (9) Both are Fundamentalists, and (10) They are all non-Protestant, Christian faiths that arose spontaneously within the last two hundred years rather than through an evolvement from any of the other denominations.

How did you do? We suspect that there were quite a few surprises, some of them truly significant. For example, many people who aren't Jewish assume (wrongly) that there are four different levels of "strictness" in Judaism. They assume that Hasidic Jews are the oldest and strictest group, that Orthodox Jews evolved from them and are somewhat less strict, that Conservative Jews evolved from *them* and are still less strict, and that Reform Jews are the newest and least strict of all. But that's quite wrong. Orthodox Jews came first, Reform Jews came next (and rejected strictness), and Conservative Jews came next (and rejected that rejection). Hasidism was founded in the eighteenth century, and is thus the oldest group, but Hasidic Jews are mystics, almost a breed apart, and did not evolve into Orthodox Jews. In fact, Hasidism had nearly died out before the advent of the later movements, and has only been reborn in the last century.

Appearances can be very deceiving, all right; similarities can mislead and confuse as much as they can educate. But in sound intellectual processing, it is necessary to consider them before going on to the next step: essential differences.

Consider the case of twins. Let's say you sit down next to a young mother in the park with a pair of identical one-year-old twins playing at her feet. You look down at them and smile; they look exactly alike. "How do you tell them apart?" you ask her.

"Oh, they don't really look alike at all," she replies. "Tim's hair is darker than Tom's, and Tom's eyes are bluer than Tim's. And Tim's fingers are plumper than Tom's, and Tom's feet are bigger than Tim's." She gestures to them. "See?"

You look down at them and smile again; they look exactly alike.

This isn't *your* mistake; it's Mom's. She's so used to the twins and has become so discerning at telling them apart that she sees small differences instead of great similarities.

We've all heard a "John Junior" say the equivalent of, "Why, I'm not like my Dad at all. It's true that we both have the same religion and we vote the same way, and we both have the same professional goals and share the same personal value system, and we enjoy similar artwork and music and follow comparable physical pursuits, but other than that, we're as different as day and night." Sometimes we're blind to what's right in front of our noses just *because* these clues are right in front of our noses.

Similarities and Differences

Essential

How well can you spot the essential differences that exist between things that are normally assumed to be very similar?

1. Well, my cat was named "Roger" until he gave birth.
2. I really can't tell Elton John from Billy Joel.
3. I have a hard time choosing professional help, like a good doctor or lawyer; for the most part, they all seem the same.
4. If I study two similar things long enough, I can begin to tell them apart.
5. If I study two similar things long enough, I can begin to tell them apart.

A "true" to number 1 is *almost* normal; it's not easy to see the gender of cats, but you should have noticed Roger was putting on weight! And a "true" to number 2? Hmm. I don't think there *is* much of a difference, although one sure has more hair now than he used to. "True" to number 3? It's normal, but that's not good enough. This is an area where understanding differences can make, well, a lot of difference in your life. A "true" to number 4 is good, and number 5 is a joke. (Or an irritation, depending on how much time you spent looking for some minuscule difference between number 5 and number 4.)

Here are more exercises and more world religions:

HINDUISM is the Western term for a 4000-year-old network of theologies to which the majority of people in India subscribe. It's polytheistic, with a divine trinity of Brahma, the creator, Vishnu, the preserver, and Shiva, the destroyer. The Veda is the most sacred scripture, culminating in the Upanishads that state the doctrine of Brahman—the absolute reality and its identity with the soul (*atman*). Hinduism is characterized by acceptance of the caste system, sacrificial ritual, and doctrines of continuing reincarnation according to one's behavior (*karma*). Escape from the reincarnation cycle with practices leading to enlightenment, including spiritual yoga, is considered the extinction (*nirvana*) of sorrow and is the goal of every Hindu.

BUDDHISM, now flourishing especially in China, was founded in India in the sixth century B.C. by Siddhārtha Gautama, later deified and known as the Buddha. The non-Vedic doctrines he preached were a kind of protestantism aimed against the monopoly of the orthodox Hindu caste of priests (Brahmans), who were proprietors of the cosmic law (*dharma*) and who alone were qualified to establish a proper relation to the gods. An ascetic, he taught meditation and advocated doctrines called the Four Noble Truths. These maintained that the cause of suffering is desire, but that desire can be overcome by an arduous Eightfold Path of moral actions. The later variation, called Zen Buddhism, also teaches that meditation can bring sudden enlightenment.

SHINTOISM is an umbrella term applied to the complex of ancient native folk beliefs of Japan. Polytheistic in a way, it has numerous desirable supernatural beings (*kami*), although not all are gods. The spirits of ancestors, great heroes, natural beauty, sex, and magical objects such as mirrors are all *kami*. Current rituals involve reverence of ancestors, pilgrimages to shrines, and celebration of festivals; however, Shinto has little theology and no congregational worship. The most important deity is the sun goddess, considered to be the ancestor of the line of emperors of Japan, each of whom was also chief priest by divine right. State Shinto was dissolved when Emperor Hirohito disavowed his divinity, but it lives on among the people.

Here are some questions:

1. Name two essential differences between Hinduism and Buddhism.
2. Name two essential differences between Buddhism and Shintoism.

No, "everything" is not an answer! We're looking for *essential* differences, not insignificant ones. Here are a few that you could have mentioned: (1) Buddhism was founded as a reaction against the authorities in orthodox Hinduism. Also, Buddhism had a living "savior," later deified, whereas Hinduism has a supernatural pantheon. (2) Buddhism has a philosophical base, and Shintoism is based on rituals. And like Hinduism, Shintoism has a supernatural pantheon of godlike entities.

Essential Differences

Looking for similarities and differences are two sides of the same coin—the coin of "discernment." We need to exercise our powers of perspicacity until they are as keen as they can be, which is very keen, indeed. Experience is all it takes, and exercise brings experience.

Let's suppose you spend the day with a new friend whom you met at the library on Saturday morning. Come Saturday night, you exchange telephone numbers and arrange to meet again at the same place the following week. As you wait on the appointed day, dozens of people stream by you into the library. Eventually, your new friend arrives, and by the time he's fifty feet away, you're already waving to him.

But suppose you spend the day watching a chimpanzee at the zoo, instead. There's a renovation the following week, and you return two weeks later to find several-dozen chimpanzees ambling around a dozen new habitats. Which one were you watching before? Can you tell? Probably not. But their caretakers can tell them apart as well as they can tell their relatives apart. How? They learn to pay attention to different things. To an entomologist, insects don't all look alike. In fact, they look wildly different. And to a botanist, leaves vary as much as flowers do. But the average person is used to paying attention to flowers and not paying attention to leaves—unless you're at a supermarket, where you're unlikely to mistake iceberg lettuce for spinach. In this case, "understanding" isn't pertinent. Simple attention is, and attention is something you can turn on at will.

Here's a nice exercise in turning on your attention and tuning in to differences. Stop by the best greengrocer or farmers' market in town and buy a small amount of each of the following: romaine lettuce, Boston lettuce, red lettuce, curly lettuce, spinach, mustard greens, sorrel, arugula, radicchio, pea shoots, and basil. (Make a set of labels ahead of time so you know which is which by the time you get back home.)

Then just before dinner, spread out everything on the kitchen table, each with its label on top. Study the way they look. Try the pea shoots first; they're very mild. Then try all the lettuces, including the radicchio. Then try the spinach, the mustard greens, the sorrel, and the arugula in that order. Save the basil for last. And don't flinch! Some of these tastes may be new to you, but each has a huge following, and for good reason.

Then try them again. Have a good time with it. Turn the labels over and see if you know which is which by the way they look. Then turn the labels back up and take fairly large amounts of several different leaves and mix them together. Close your eyes and take a bite of one of them. Which is it? Open your eyes to check, and if you aren't sure, compare the looks of what's left of that leaf to the greens that are still labeled. Stay with it until you've cleared away a few cobwebs from the abilities you left back in college. And then mix everything together in a big bowl and call me. I'll bring the olive oil and balsamic vinegar.

We're back to the exercises now, and we're going to close this chapter with a little yin and yang:

CONFUCIANISM is often called a religion, but it began as a system of ethical principles for the guidance of society, based on the practice of kindheartedness and demonstrated in a combination of etiquette and ritual. Its origins lie in the collection of sayings known as the Analects, attributed to Confucius, who lived in the sixth century B.C. A sage rather than a prophet, Confucius possessed a keen sense of morality—which he spoke of as a heavenly force—but he seldom discussed traditional religion. When asked about the worship of supernatural spirits, he said, "We don't know yet how to serve men. How can we know about serving the spirits?"

Considering this, Confucius was an original thinker and maybe even a revolutionary one—although he didn't represent himself as such. Instead, his deep conviction of the native dignity of all men made him very well loved. "In education," he said, "there are no class distinctions." His pleasing personality, however, may have been another factor in his popularity. Combined with a talent for succinct comments that embraced important concepts, Confucius had a sense of mission, and for more than two millennia, his thinking has served as the official, and unofficial, creed of the Chinese people, many of whom go so far as to call it a state religion. Remember the saying, "Do unto others what you would have them do unto you"? Confucius wrote it twenty-five hundred years ago, and it still sounds pretty wise today.

TAOISM, another philosophical and religious system, has been second in importance only to Confucianism in China. The philosophical system comes from a book called the *Tao te Ching*, which is attributed to Lao-tzu but was likely written in the third century B.C. Taoists condemned the social virtues as outlined by Confucius as excessive interference in the life of the individual; instead, Taoism—which is named after its central idea, Tao, or The Way—emphasizes an eternal creative process that follows a doctrine of absolute noninterference. That is, just as it is the nature of a bird to fly and the destiny of a flower to live only for a day, man is happiest and most free when he lives according to his own nature and his own destiny, avoiding anxiety about life and death, and rising above gain and loss. In large part, Taoism contributed to the Chinese love of nature and sense of serenity. Later, it adopted a fully developed religious system for people who didn't feel adequately fulfilled by the ethical system of Confucianism.

Here, to end the chapter, is just one more question:

3. Name one essential difference between Confucianism and Taoism.

There are many, but here is the essence: (3) Confucianism is down-to-earth, practical, and full of advice on how to get through your day and live your life. On the other hand, Taoism is mystical, lyrical, and abounds with gentle counsel about finding the path to such things as harmony and everlasting peace.

So you're ready to move to China, right? (We are, too!) But as we don't know anyone who'll deliver pizza that far, we'll settle for where we are, at least for now. All food is very similar—it's all nourishment. But it's very different, too. When you're in the mood for chop suey, a hamburger looks terrible; and when you're in the mood for a hamburger, chop suey looks terrible. Everything may be made of the same basic "stuff," but as the French say, *vive la différence.*

If you're a chemist, knowing the difference between an oxygen atom and a hydrogen atom is important. Where would modern science be if chemists shrugged their shoulders and said, "Oh, all atoms are pretty much alike." (Just thumb through your college chemistry book. They *do* look pretty much alike.) And what about astronomers? What's the difference between one star and another, anyway? Or physics. A force is a force is a force, right? And what if doctors didn't bother with all those specific diagnoses and simply classified all pathologies as "just feeling lousy"? Aspirin would be the only drug on the drugstore shelves.

And in human terms, knowing how we are similar to everyone else allows us to formulate codes of human decency; knowing how we are different is how we can make our lives fulfilling. As Confucius said, "By nature all men are pretty much alike; it is by custom and habit that they are set apart."

Uh-oh. It's just occurred to us how much we like Chinese take-out. Can you imagine how good it must be *there?*

BOOK ELEVEN

Using Analogies
Standard (To Explain)

How well do you see analogies?

1. Because of analogies, my intelligence test score was a negative number.
2. If they're easy, I can figure them out; but they can get pretty obscure, you know.
3. I like them on tests, but I don't see how they relate to the real world.
4. I use analogies and even metaphors and similes. On a good day, I sound like a voiceover from a bad detective film.
5. Considering the interconnectedness of all things, all the possibilities available in an analogy are equally valid.

Did you answer "true" to number 1? We sympathize; some people dislike analogies. "True" to number 2? That's probably the reason for number 1; but don't worry—we'll be very straightforward in this chapter. And "true" to number 3? The coming pages will show you the error of your ways! And to number 4, too? You don't sound like Bogart or Bacall, do you? If so, would you mind recording our answering-machine message for us? "True" to number 5? That's okay; one needs a little interconnectedness every now and zen.

Try timing yourself in this chapter with the coming exercises—all taken from the subject of political science.

Here are some systems of government that have been practiced by one nation or another over the course of history. These two are monocratic (rule by a single person or party):

MONARCHY: Rule by a hereditary sovereign like a king or emperor. A monarch may be an absolute ruler or little more than a ceremonial dignitary. In modern times, countries such as Great Britain, Denmark, and The Netherlands maintain a monarch as the ceremonial head of state, and although s/he is an essential figure in all important official occasions and a symbol of national unity, s/he is almost entirely without real power.

TOTALITARIANISM: Absolute rule by a dictator, whether a single individual or a single party. While monarchies (with the head of state legitimized by birth) have virtually vanished from contemporary life, totalitarian governments (with the head of state legitimized by force) now flourish. In some countries, the head of state consolidated personal power by banning opposition parties; in other countries, the army seized power and established a military dictatorship.

In general, a monarchy is considered to be the "rightist" form of monocratic government; totalitarianism usually calls itself the "leftist" form of monocratic government. Some modern examples of the latter are communism, fascism, and nazism. ("Nazism" is the contraction for national socialism.)

These three are democratic (rule by the entire population) systems of government:

DEMOCRACY: Government by the entire population of a state. This form of government was viewed dimly by the Greek philosophers Socrates and Aristotle, and democracy in ancient Athens excluded the majority of people from participation. The eighteenth-century philosopher Rousseau, however, argued that the success of democracy depended on such things as an austere style of life and equality of social rank. The democracies of the modern second and third worlds focus on equality and express little interest in legal rights; the Western democracies emphasize more formal rights.

REPUBLIC: Government by a small group of people elected by the population of a state. The Roman Republic balanced elements of a monarchy, an aristocracy, and a democracy—a mix now considered to be a fundamental part of classical republicanism. The United States itself was established as a republic, and this form of government was "guaranteed" in the Constitution. The founders believed that laws, rather than popular approval, should be the final authority, and (contrary to common belief) the word "democracy" does not appear in the Declaration of Independence, the U.S. Constitution, or in the first state constitutions.

ANARCHY: The absence of any coercive government at all. Anarchists are varied, most seeming to have little in common except their definition of a common political enemy—government itself. They believe in a society in which personal freedom is at a maximum—even though a price surely will be paid for it. (Right-wing anarchists are the radical fringe of the Libertarians, who hold a strong doctrine of individual rights and believe that the most desirable social and economic system is capitalism unhampered by most government restrictions.)

Here are a few analogies. (Choose one answer only.)

1. KING is to MONARCHY as _____ is to TOTALITARIANISM.
   (A) EMPEROR, (B) SOVEREIGN, (C) DICTATOR, or (D) THE POPULATION
2. MONARCHY is to RIGHTIST as _____ is to LEFTIST.
   (A) COMMUNISM, (B) FASCISM, (C) NAZISM, or (D) TOTALITARIANISM
3. ENTIRE POPULATION is to DEMOCRACY as _____ are to REPUBLIC.
   (A) FOUNDING FATHERS, (B) ELECTED REPRESENTATIVES, or (C) LAWS.
4. REPRESENTATION is to REPUBLIC as _____ is/are to DEMOCRACY.
   (A) ENTIRE POPULATION, (B) DIRECT PARTICIPATION, or (C) CITIZENS.
5. RIGHT-WING ANARCHISTS are to LIBERTARIANISM as _____ is/are to TOTALITARIANISM. (Hint: the radical fringe.)
   (A) DICTATORS, (B) COMMUNISTS, (C) FASCISTS, or (D) NAZIS.

And here are the answers: (1) C, (2) D, (3) B, (4) A, and (5) D.

Any trouble with those? (Getting three out of five right is good.) We'll bet you had to stop and think more than you thought you would. The concepts are easy enough (although some of the information may have surprised you) but getting through each analogy was like running through the shallow end of the pool, right? If so, that means you got plenty of mental exercise. That is, (ideally), the exercises themselves should *be* fairly easy, but *feel* difficult.

Standard Analogies

Anyone who has ever taken a test is surely familiar with analogies, but I personally find them more helpful as an instructional device than as a testing device. That is, I find more value in their uncluttered presentation of relationships than in their ability to fit into a very small space—which is probably why we find them so often on tests. But either way, the ability to see relationships is tremendously valuable to the intellect, and even if we don't find any written analogies outside of formal tests, we need to learn to create them ourselves as a bridge to the perspective that we so often lack. When we cite the excesses of the radical fringe of the "other side," we must remember the excesses of "our own."

Great thinkers often rely on analogies to transmit their points, and more ordinary writers often learn to use analogies as well, even if only in their work. After all, what are metaphors and similes if not forms of analogy? For better or for worse, it sometimes appears that there is a long-standing literary tradition for the writer not to describe things as they are, but rather to compare them to other things. Literature is filled with such analogies—from crime fiction ("She was hanging all over me like a cheap suit,") to love sonnets ("Shall I compare thee to a summer's day?") to everything in between ("Shall I compare thee to a cheap suit?"). Why do writers persist in this sort of thing? Because the more mature and profound the analogy, the more mature and profound the writer and his or her work is considered.

And even less literary writers use analogy to great effect. When communicating a thought—be it on the nature of subatomic particles or a passionate love affair—it can be very helpful to appeal to a broader range of information in order to better convey the point. If you write, "He had blue eyes," this isn't going to satisfy anyone, except maybe an employee of the Department of Motor Vehicles. But if you write lines like, "His blue eyes radiated the intensity of a lightning bolt destroying an electrical power substation," your novel will have more effect. (Although the effect may be no more than a prospective editor running your manuscript through the shredder rather than mailing it back to you.)

Probably the best way to handle analogies is to use them. That is, don't look at them as something you find on a test. Instead, begin to use analogies in your everyday life. Make them a tool of comprehension (and communication) rather than one of testing.

But remember not to allow analogies to limit you. They should bring understanding and a greater perspective, not a sort of artificially induced equivalence. We may find that A is analogous to B in one sense or in two or three or more while it is different in others, but just because we find differences between A and B doesn't mean that the analogies are incorrect. Instead, it simply means that A isn't *equal* to B, which we presumably knew already. In brief, analogies should be tools, not excuses.

Here are more exercises.

The following two are economic "isms" that are so passionately held in the Western world that they have begun to take on political meaning:

CAPITALISM: An economic system in which privately owned enterprises compete in a free market with little governmental interference. Capitalism has become the political principle of choice for those who believe that unburdened competition by free individuals produces the finest product, whether that product is hospitals or shoes, and that the economic well-being of the state will be felt by most deserving citizens, if not all. Neither economic nor social inequality is capitalism's goal, and individual responsibility for one's own lot in life is considered essential. Capitalism has been most forcefully attacked by those who maintain that the personal ambition of some people will bring about the exploitation of those who are less able.

SOCIALISM: A group of related systems that use economic means to achieve social goals, the most common element being an emphasis on the welfare of the group rather than the individual. Socialism's proponents believe that the credit for providing goods and services cannot be claimed by any individual, because production is the result of the labor of a group, and so government should take the role of allocating the rewards of production to the whole of society. Karl Marx's dictum, "From each according to his abilities, to each according to his needs," illustrates the aim of replacing individualism with a form of community (as in "communist") production and distribution. (Marx was the father of communism.)

And here's one more "ism" for you, a self-explanatory one:

CRITICISM: The socialist opponents of capitalism charge that capitalism is inherently tolerant of class distinction and economic inequality, and they believe socialism will (or should) replace selfishness with altruism, and competition with cooperation, in accordance with often-quoted religious ideals.

The capitalist opponents of socialism charge that socialism ignores human nature and that the competition of the free market is what generates progress. They also hold a fundamental belief that individuals merit reward through their own personal initiative and industriousness rather than through the demonstration of need.

Here are a few more questions:

1. PRIVATE OWNERSHIP is to CAPITALISM as _____ is to SOCIALISM.
   (A) FREE MARKET, (B) COMMON MARKET, or (C) PUBLIC OWNERSHIP
2. COMPETITION is to CAPITALISM as _____ is to SOCIALISM.
   (A) COOPERATION, (B) EXPLOITATION, (C) ALTRUISM, or (D) OPPRESSION
3. MOTIVATION is to CAPITALISM as _____ is to SOCIALISM.
   (A) DEMAND, (B) DESIRE, (C) NEED, or (D) PERSONAL INITIATIVE
4. INDIVIDUAL is to CAPITALISM as _____ is to SOCIALISM.
   (A) UNDERPRIVILEGED, (B) PRIVILEGED, (C) OVERPRIVILEGED, or (D) GROUP
5. THE DESERVING are to CAPITALISM as _____ are to SOCIALISM.
   (A) THE OPPRESSED, (B) THE NEEDY, or (C) ALL CITIZENS

And here are the answers: (1) C, (2) A, (3) C, (4) D, and (5) C. (Three correct is good.)

Analogies are indispensable in teaching and understanding, and they are used in a broad spectrum of disciplines. If you've studied chemistry, you've read that atomic structure is "like a mini-solar system" and that electrons orbit the nucleus "like planets." If you've studied biology, you've read that the human eye works "like a camera." (And if you've studied photography, you've read that a camera works "like the human eye"!)

So understanding relationships shouldn't be considered a test of knowledge—although it certainly can be used in that fashion. Instead, understanding relationships is a way to grasp understanding itself, a way to get perspective, and in the case of politics in particular, a way to find out where we're going *before* we get there and have our noses pressed firmly up against it.

As you know, we're not attempting to teach political science in this chapter; instead, we're just using it to pinpoint and exercise a particular mental ability. But think of the educational opportunity wasted if we were to use "up is to down" and "black is to white" as examples of analogies. The information you read was easy to understand and remember, and any difficulty you experienced in the above analogies illustrates another point—an extremely important one for the purposes of this book. If you're just a passive receiver of the news, you'd better make sure that you get a thorough grasp of the historical context, implications, and ramifications of your ideas before your vote. Otherwise, kiddo, you're not just irresponsible; you're dangerous.

Using Analogies

Opposite (To Understand)

How well do you see opposite analogies?

1. The only things I'm grasping right now are straws.
2. I find standard analogies easier than opposite ones.
3. I find opposite analogies easier than standard ones.
4. I like anything that's multiple choice—especially analogies. I detest "essay" tests.
5. I was pretty good at the standard analogies because of my sense of cosmic harmony and the interconnectedness of everything, but I'm afraid I'm going to have a hard time with opposites. Maybe I should just read the rest of the chapter and then go and meditate in the bathtub the way I usually do.

A "true" to number 1? We know you're kidding. But an answer of "true" to number 2 is normal, and so is "false" to number 3. "True" to number 4 probably means you have some performance anxiety, a perfectly understandable and reasonable phenomenon, and/or that you're less comfortable expressing yourself than others. (And those "others" always gain points on essay tests, don't they?) "True" to number 5? Don't turn on the water yet! This section will be right up your alley. Think of the pleasure you'll get when you find harmony among *opposites!*

Here are more exercises:

These are the two ideological poles considered "rightist" and "leftist." But first be aware that "conservatism" ("rightist") and "liberalism" ("leftist") as political philosophies mean something very different from the use of "conservative" and "liberal" as relative terms to describe an existing political situation. Confusing them, which is unfortunately all too common for such important concepts, is destructive to our political understanding and has serious consequences on our ability to make wise political choices. If we're unaware of the real differences between the terms, we may vote for the opposite of what we actually want.

"Conservatism" is a "rightist" political philosophy that now has much in common with capitalism and began as we'll describe below. "Liberalism" is a "leftist" political philosophy that now has much in common with socialism and began as we'll describe below, also. But when "conservative" and "liberal" are applied to an existing political situation (which may be "rightest" or "leftist" or anything else), they mean something different. The "conservative" element is the group that wants things to remain the same. The "liberal" element is the group that wants a change. In Moscow, for example, the people who wanted to *keep* the leftist government were called "conservatives"; the people who wanted to *change* the leftist government were called "liberals."

CONSERVATISM: Conservatism began at the beginning of the nineteenth century as a reaction to the French Revolution and its demands for social and political change. Defenders of the older values formulated their own political and social theories in opposition to the new ones. Conservatism was further strengthened by the emergence of socialism in the nineteenth century; fear of this radical new movement began to swell the numbers of conservatives, who were unwavering opponents of socialism. In the twentieth century, even more people embraced conservatism in dismay over the success of the Russian Revolution.

LIBERALISM: Although it defies scholarly description, we might say that modern liberalism also began with the French Revolution and its ultimate conversion of an aristocratic society into a more democratic one. Liberalism was also responsible for the Russian Revolution. Since the middle of the twentieth century, both the two major political parties in the United States might well be described as liberal, as both are sensitive to the ever-changing interests of the entire population. However, Republicans typically favor less government overall, while Democrats favor more government in general.

In the United States and throughout much of the modern world, liberalism is the foremost political doctrine, generating others such as socialism, communism, fascism, and even nazism—a case of socialism gone so horribly awry as to destroy even its own liberal institutions in its quest for social control.

Here are a few opposite analogies and one special note: We've purposely distinguished "conservatism/liberalism" from "conservative/liberal" here, in order to illustrate our point about the two very different meanings of these terms with a common derivation. However, you won't find this kind of distinction in the newspaper. The terms are most often used interchangeably—even though that usage is commonly misleading. In your everyday reading, then, you'll need to distinguish them for yourself, but this has already been done here, so that you can better see our point. (By the way, these are going to be far more challenging.)

1. LEFTIST is to RIGHTIST as _____ is to CONSERVATISM.
   (A) CONSERVATIVE, (B) LIBERAL, (C) LIBERALISM, (D) LIBERTARIAN
2. CONSERVATIVE is to LIBERAL as _____ is to DIFFERENT.
   (A) INDIFFERENT, (B) DISINTERESTED, (C) UNUSUAL, or (D) SAME
3. ARISTOCRACY is to FRENCH REVOLUTION as _____ is to LIBERALISM.
   (A) CONSERVATISM, (B) CONSERVATIONISM, (C) CONSERVATORY

We're feeling a little guilty about having just called these challenging, so we'll call the following a "bonus question" instead.

4. REPUBLICAN is to DEMOCRAT as _____ is to SOCIAL CONTROL.
   (A) SOCIAL WORK, (B) SOCIAL STUDIES, or (C) SOCIAL INTEREST
5. LIBERAL is to 1917 RUSSIA as _____ is to 1992 RUSSIA.
   (A) LIBERAL, (B) CONSERVATIVE, or (C) CONSERVATIONIST.

Here are the answers: (1) C, (2) D, (3) A, (4) C, and (5) A.

Opposite Analogies

We apologize for the bonus questions (but not too much). Here's an explanation: We said REPUBLICAN is to DEMOCRAT as SOCIAL INTEREST is to SOCIAL CONTROL, because Republicans like to see government eschew active encouragement of social goals for its citizens, but Democrats like to legislate them. And we said LIBERAL is to 1917 RUSSIA as LIBERAL is to 1992 RUSSIA, because the people who fought to overthrow the monarchists were called liberals (because they had popular approval to reject the established order), but the people who fought to overthrow the communists were *also* called liberals (for that same reason). Their politics were very different.

Standard analogies are useful both in teaching and understanding, but opposite analogies force more intellectual exercise with their "compare and contrast" methodology. Much of this exercise was in taking each possible answer and "trying it out" in the blank, doing this repeatedly until you decided on the correct fit—a method that applies to both standard and opposite analogies, of course. But you can get even more out of the exercises. Don't just tabulate your score. Instead, wherever you had a wrong answer, take the correct one and analyze *why* it's correct. And try hard not to be defensive of your own answer.

(Forget your politics for the moment! You wouldn't want us to write this chapter with an uncritical acceptance of whatever political ideas happen to be in vogue, would you? You *would?!*)

Back to the exercises:

The following is a brief explanation of the confusion that arises when reading and using the words "Democratic" (capitalized) versus "democratic" (not capitalized), the words "Republican" versus "republican," and the words "democracy" and "republic" in general. The "democratic" words are not synonymous, and neither are the "republican" words, and the "democratic" words are very commonly misunderstood.

Both Democrats and Republicans alike believe in modern "democracy," a concept of government in which the important policy decisions are directed by a majority of the adult citizens. Likewise, they both believe in the modern "republic," a form of government in which the head of state is not a monarch, and the ruling power resides in the citizens entitled to vote, exercised by elected officials who are accountable to them and who govern according to law. A democracy may not always be a republic, and a republic may not always be a democracy. However, our country is both—a democratic republic (or a republican democracy).

"Democrats" as people often characterize themselves by their desire for social and economic equality. "Republicans" as people often characterize themselves by their rejection of government as a social and economic power.

And this is where the confusion arises: The (uncapitalized) word "democratic," when used to refer to the concept of "democracy," doesn't have anything more to do with the Democrats than it does with the Republicans. *Both* parties believe in democracy. Only when the word "Democratic" is capitalized and used in reference to party politics does it refer to one group and not the other.

Here are eight words we should understand:

democracy	a concept of power in government
democratic	referring to the above
republic	a structural form of government
republican	referring to the above
Democrat	a member of one political party
Democratic	referring to the above
Republican	a member of another political party
Republican	referring to the above

Here are the last two exercises on analogies. (Don't worry; the above looks harder than it is. We know we used up your limit of patience on the last group.)

1. "democracy" is to "republic" as _____ is to "republican"
   (A) democracy, (B) democratic, (C) Democrat, (C) Democratic
2. "Democrat" is to "Republican" as _____ is to "Republican"
   (A) democracy, (B) democratic, (C) Democrat, (D) Democratic

And here are the answers: (1) B, and (2) C.

Now you know the truth. That *was* hard! We were afraid to tell you ahead of time, because we were worried that you might just give up and go meditate in the bathtub.

Say, that isn't water we hear running, is it?

Shakespeare, of course, was one of the masters of comparing and contrasting. Remember how he compared his love to a summer's day? In Sonnet 130, he writes the following:

My mistress' eyes are nothing like the sun;
Coral is far more red than her lips' red;

If snow be white, why then her breasts are dun;
If hairs be wires, black wires grow on her head.
I have seen roses damasked, red and white,
But no such roses see I in her cheeks;
And in some perfumes is there more delight
Than in the breath that from my mistress reeks.

We've all had bad dates, but *really!* First, there's the sun (which her eyes are nothing like, maybe a plus in a crowded movie theater); then there's coral (which isn't red, but apparently better than no lip color at all); then there's snow (which makes her overall complexion look like dishwater); and then her head appears to be sprouting wires instead of hair (oh, those early perms were the pits, all right). And as if that weren't enough, the woman even has bad breath!

No romance whatsoever. Or so it would seem. But the final couplet holds the following sentiment:

And yet, by heaven, I think my love as rare
As any she belied with false compare.

Doggone it, the big lunk loves her anyway! (Excuse us. We're going to find a handkerchief and have a good cry.)

BOOK TWELVE

Sequence Arrangement

Logical

Are you a logical person? How logical?

1. I really don't even *like* logical order. I like chaos, instead. It makes life so much more unpredictable and exciting.
2. I could be more logical, I guess, but I don't like doing something because "it makes sense." Maybe I'm still a little rebellious.
3. I try to use logic wherever I know how, but that "Which came first, the chicken or the egg?" question reminds me of how much stuff can't be handled with logic, anyway.
4. I'm *too* ordered. Running out of an item I need is unimaginable to me. I mean, when you're down to your last box of staples, you go out and buy some more, right?
5. I'm pretty good about logic and order. But I drop it the moment it ceases to be useful and becomes an end in itself.

An answer of "true" to number 1 is just fine, but what a mess your apartment must be! And "true" to number 2 and number 3 is normal. A "true" to number 4 is "less" normal, but so what? As long as you're not compulsive, you're probably very efficient. But a "false" to number 5 may indicate a psychological problem.

We'll start with some exercises from the subject of twentieth-century world history.

These are a few of the events of WORLD WAR I:

The mood in Europe was extremely tense; Germany was arming and not hiding its moves. In 1914, Archduke Ferdinand of Austria-Hungary was shot by a Serbian anarchist; Austria blamed Serbia and declared war. Russia mobilized to aid the Serbs; Germany did the same for Austria-Hungary. A German invasion of Belgium failed to capture Russia's ally France, and Germany's ally Italy switched to the opposition. Japan became involved in order to seize German possessions in the Far East. Russia was brought to its knees by its Revolution, and its new leader, Lenin, accepted Germany's conditions for peace; Germany could now focus on the Western front. Angered by attacks on American merchant ships, the United States joined the war against Germany. In 1918, Germany conceded defeat and signed an armistice. At the Paris Peace Conference, the victorious side redrew the map of Europe, although the U.S. refused to ratify the Treaty of Versailles. Lenin died and was succeeded by Stalin; in the new German republic, Hitler began his rise.

Here are a few of those events again, but out of order. Put them back in logical order:

A. Germany signed an armistice, ending the war.
B. The victorious side redrew the map of Europe.
C. Archduke Ferdinand was shot.
D. The U.S. refused to ratify the Treaty of Versailles.
E. A German invasion of Belgium failed to capture France.

Here are a few more events. Put them back in logical order:

F. Lenin died and was succeeded by Stalin.
G. Lenin accepted Germany's conditions for peace.
H. Russia, committed to aid the Serbs, mobilized.
I. The Russian Revolution brought Lenin to power.

These are a few of the events of THE TWENTIES AND THIRTIES:

Congress raised tariffs, closed the door to immigrants, and insisted on the repayment of war debts; with new prosperity, the twenties began to roar. Wild investment in stocks produced a great bull market unrelated to the earning capacity of the economy. In 1929, prices on the New York Stock Exchange dropped sharply; banks and businesses went broke; factories shut down. The Wall Street crash echoed around the world, devastating countries whose economies had depended on American loans; Latin America and Central Europe were reduced to poverty. Economies ruined by the war were virtually destroyed, and budding dictators courted the frightened, unknowing masses. In the thrall of promises of benevolence and socialism, the people of Italy gave control to Mussolini, and the Germans gave it to Hitler.

Put the following events back in logical order:

J. Prices on the New York Stock Exchange dropped sharply.
K. Wild investment in stocks produced a great bull market.
L. Banks and businesses went broke.
M. The Wall Steet crash echoed around the world.
N. With new prosperity, the twenties began to roar.

Here are the answers: (1) C, (2) E, (3) A, (4) B, (5) D, (6) H, (7) I, (8) G, (9) F, (10) N, (11) K, (12) J, (13) L, and (14) M.

You didn't need an encyclopedic knowledge of World War I and the Great Depression to order these events logically, but you didn't put them in order instantly either, did you? Regardless of the familiarity of these events, you had to stop and think, right? Good. That's the exercise.

Logical Sequence Arrangement

As you know, chronological order merely places events in order according to when they occurred. But just because an ordering system is chronological doesn't mean that it's logical. If you were organizing books in a library, you could certainly stack them all in the order of publication date, but few people would have the time to make fruitful use of such a library.

Nature is chronological, but humankind is not. Rather, we do most things in life in some kind of logical order—regardless of whether we quite realize it. It makes no sense to brush your teeth *before* a meal, does it? Or to wash your hands *before* going to bury your ex-wife in the garden? And even "illogical order" is logical. Somehow, it seems silly to buy a burglar alarm *after* we've been robbed, but in another way, it makes perfectly good sense.

It's difficult to make suggestions about how to think logically, but here's one, anyway: Most logic is a form of mathematical reasoning, and we can gain expertise in it by using natural inclination and/or experience. But when real-life situations take the place of numbers, we can easily mistake chronological order for logical order, ruining our conclusions without our even knowing it. This kind of faulty reasoning can even reverse cause and effect.

Here's an example: How often have you heard the statement, "Fish developed gills so they could breathe under water"? That makes no sense. It implies that fish who *couldn't* breathe underwater made a decision to develop gills so they *could*. Instead, gilled fish are a passive *effect* of natural selection rather than an active *cause* of it. That is, fish didn't select gills at all; rather, the water "selected" *them* by being inhospitable to creatures without an underwater survival mechanism. It would be more accurate to say, "Conditions under water resulted in the development of gills on fish."

The first time I heard that "fish story," I envisioned a fish lying on the shore and saying to its wife, "Yep, gills are the answer, all right. Why, we'd be able to spend all our time down there having fun, instead of the aggravation of having to bob to the surface constantly. I'll be right in the middle of gulping down one of the kids for lunch when I've got to go back up *again*. I mean, by the end of the day, I'm just exhausted, you know?"

And she replies, "That does it, Charley. I'm leaving. Go ahead with your stupid gills. I'm going to get *myself* a pair of *legs*." (Okay, okay. So she was probably a "fishwife.")

Here are more exercises:

These are a few of the events of WORLD WAR II:

Germany invaded Poland in 1939; committed to aid Poland, Britain and France declared war on Germany. German troops overran most of Scandinavia and northern France; France surrendered. Meanwhile, Italy joined Germany; Britain continued to resist. Germany overran Greece and Yugoslavia, then invaded the U.S.S.R. In 1941, Japan bombed Pearl Harbor; the United States and Britain declared war on Japan; Germany and Italy declared war on the U.S. In 1944, Allied troops landed in Normandy and drove back the opposition; German troops occupied Brussels, Warsaw, and Budapest. The Allies crossed the Rhine; the Soviets occupied Vienna and headed for Berlin, where Hitler committed suicide; in 1945, Germany surrendered. The U.S. dropped atom bombs on Hiroshima and Nagasaki; Japan surrendered. After the war, Soviet troops occupied nearly all Central and Eastern European capitals; Germany was divided. Soviet domination of the East and American "domination" of the West created the Cold War.

Put the following events back in logical order:

A. Hitler committed suicide in Berlin.
B. German troops overran most of Scandinavia and northern France.
C. The Allies crossed the Rhine.
D. Germany invaded Poland in 1939.
E. In 1944, Allied troops landed in Normandy.
F. Committed to aid Poland, Britain and France declared war.

And put the following events back in logical order:

G. The U.S. dropped atom bombs on Hiroshima and Nagasaki.
H. The United States and Britain declared war on Japan.
I. Germany and Italy declared war on the U.S.
J. Japan bombed Pearl Harbor.
K. Japan surrendered.

Here are a few of the events of the COLD WAR:

The struggle between East and West, between Communism/Socialism and Democracy/Capitalism, generated continuing conflicts in the world. In 1950, Communist North Korea attacked South Korea; the United Nations intervened with American troops and drove the North Koreans back behind the Chinese border. In 1954, Communists in Vietnam took the North from France; a pro-American government took the South. In the 1960's, North Vietnam's Communist guerrillas were about to conquer the South, when U.S. troops were sent to oppose them; a war unpopular in America ensued. In 1973, mounting pressure caused the U.S. to withdraw from South Vietnam; in 1975, the Communists took over all of Vietnam. Growing nuclear arsenals of the two superpowers caused increasing concern to citizens and leaders worldwide, but eventually the economic failure of communism/socialism caused U.S.S.R. President Mikhail Gorbachev to begin westernizing the Soviet Union; he and U.S. President Ronald Reagan signed disarmament treaties. In 1989, the Berlin Wall—the symbol of the Cold War—was torn down; Germany was reunited. Soviet satellites began to break away one by one—starting with Yugoslavia, Hungary, and Romania. In 1991, the U.S.S.R. was dissolved into the Confederation of Independent States.

Put the following events back in logical order:

L. **The U.S.S.R. was dissolved into the Confederation of Independent States.**

M. **The economic failure of communism/socialism caused Gorbachev to begin westernizing the country; he and Reagan signed disarmament treaties.**

N. **Communist guerrillas were about to take South Vietnam when American troops were sent to oppose them; a war unpopular in America ensued.**

O. **The Berlin Wall—the symbol of the Cold War—was torn down; Germany was reunited.**

P. **Mounting pressure caused the U.S. to withdraw from South Vietnam; two years later, the Communists took over the country.**

And here are the answers: (1) D, (2) F, (3) B, (4) E, (5) C, (6) A, (7) J, (8) H, (9) I, (10) G, (11) K, (12) N, (13) P, (14) M, (15) O, and (16) L.

How did you do?

Thinking logically means thinking like a detective. Let's say a pickled herring has disappeared from a suburban home, and you're called to reconstruct the events that led to the crime. You arrive and take note of the suspicious looks being exchanged by the soon-to-be estranged husband and his wife seated across from each other at the dinner table, the constant complaining of his mother-in-law in the rocking chair, the nihilistic attitude of the teenage son, and the stomach rumblings of the large cat attempting to conceal itself behind the refrigerator. Hmm.

You pick up the cat—herring breath! The teenage boy and the old lady exchange meaningful glances. You pry her little fist open and find another herring. The boy starts to bolt from the room, but he trips over the cat and falls; a third herring pops out of his trouser pocket. The wife bends over and tries to grab it from the floor before anyone can see it, and a fourth herring falls out of her bosom. "I should have known!" cries the husband, standing. "You're all in this together!"

Oops. We've begun to wander into fiction; we apologize. Thinking logically is serious business, and we know that. Here's a question that's been debated for centuries: Which came first, the chicken or the egg? And here's an answer, straight from logic:

The egg came first. A chicken is not defined by the kind of egg it lays. (A horse is a horse even if it gives birth to a mule.) But an egg is defined by the kind of creature it contains. (An egg that contains a robin is a "robin" egg, no matter what laid it.)

Therefore, if you believe in evolution, at some point a creature that was almost a chicken laid an egg that contained a chicken, and as an egg is defined by the kind of creature it contains, the egg came first.

That's logical. But it happens to be chronological, too—which is one of the reasons that the two are sometimes confused. And that brings us to the next half of the chapter, of course.

Sequence
Arrangement
Chronological

O_r are you a "chronological" person instead?

1. I don't know. The binding on my page-a-day calendar broke, and I had a hard time putting the days back in order.
2. I've noticed that these questions are in logical *and* chronological order. Does that count?
3. No problem. I determine chronological order by simple logic without having to resort to rote memorization.
4. I do fairly well as long as events unfold like the plot of a mystery novel.
5. Chronological order? I thrive on it. Anything out of order is disturbing. I can't even bear to watch *Citizen Kane.*

A "true" to number 1? Don't worry about it; we have a page-a-day calendar that doesn't have the month on each page, too. A "true" to number 2 is nice, but a "true" to number 3 isn't. We *told* you not to confuse logical order and chronological order! (As an example, take the political events in the year immediately preceding a presidential election. See how illogical chronological order can be?) A "true" to number 4 is very good, and a "true" to number 5 is understandable. But don't ever bother reading *The Time Machine.*

Here are some exercises from the timeline of important periods in Western civilization—including several "Golden Ages."

These are some of the earliest in history:

MESOPOTAMIA (4500–600 B.C.), the "cradle of civilization," is now known as the Middle East and has a turbulent history. The Sumerians created one of the first civilizations—whose achievements included the first codes of law, extensive use of writing, schools and libraries, and the use of gold and silver as money. The Babylonians conquered the Sumerians and added the foundations of grammar, mathematics, medicine, astronomy, and philosophy. Their Code of Hammurabi established the law of punishment according to the crime: "an eye for an eye, a tooth for a tooth."

EGYPT (3500–600 B.C.) was "the gift of the Nile," and the people who settled there built not only the pyramids, but also a culture that was the master of the Mediterranean world. They advanced both the arts and the sciences, and their agricultural system—which made use of extensive systems of irrigation—created a surplus through which trade with others made Egypt a wealthy civilization. Toward the end of the Empire, however, both Egypt's people and its rulers became servile to its priests, and the subsequent stagnation left it vulnerable to conquest.

GREECE (1000–300 B.C.) The Western world's Greek legacy shows itself in nearly every aspect of modern life—from our forms of literature to our forms of athletics, including the Olympic Games. From the Greeks came our systems of business and finance and our systems of schools and universities. To the Greeks, we owe the essential techniques of mining, engineering, and the foundations of calculus and trigonometry, not to mention the perfection of three-dimensional geometry. And because of the Greeks, medicine, chemistry, astronomy, and physics took giant leaps forward.

ROME (500 B.C.–A.D. 300) conquered Greece, then assimilated its culture. Although the Romans did not advance the sciences, they went on to achieve unsurpassed progress in the art of government—including the establishment of a republic of free men and a system of law that safeguarded the lives and property of most Europeans and gave incentive to industry. Banking and investment, state-supported education, and even plumbing and sanitation all evolved from the Romans. Why did the Roman Empire decline and fall? Some blame corruption and violence, but others point to its ethical structure and the growing influence of the new religion called Christianity.

THE MIDDLE AGES (300–1300) began with the fall of the Roman Empire, the spread of Christianity, and the rise of the first Christian emperor. Vast hordes of barbarians swept across Europe, but by the late 700's, church and state were unified, and the Holy Roman Empire took shape. In Northern Europe, England, Ireland, France, and Germany began to emerge from the ashes. After the Crusades opened trade routes, an economic revolution began that stimulated business and industry and the beginnings of capitalism.

Here are the names of the above five civilizations again. All we want you to do is put them in chronological order. (Surprise!)

(A) Middle Ages, (B) Rome, (C) Egypt, (D) Mesopotamia, and (E) Greece

---

Chronological Sequence Arrangement

"Chrono" logic makes sense, as do other kinds of logic, but only within a certain band of understanding. In retrospect, one can see what happened to great civilizations and, to a much smaller extent, why. But for us to assume that those changes represent anything logical, purposeful, or even desirable, would be an error. The inexorable restraints imposed by the arrow of time will thwart the greatest design.

As Marcus Aurelius Antoninus said:

Time is a sort of river of passing events, and strong is its current; no sooner is a thing brought to sight than it is swept by, and another takes its place, and this too will be swept away.

Here's a way to get a better grasp of the difference between "chrono" logic and deductive/inductive logic. Following is a capsule description of each of the civilizations we just reviewed. Don't try too hard to recognize them, okay?

A. vast hordes of barbarians roam Northern Europe, church and state unified, religious crusades opened trade routes, new countries emerge from chaos, economic revolution begins
B. little science, but advanced the art of government, safeguarded lives and property, developed banking and invest-

ment, state-supported education, and plumbing and
sanitation

C. advanced both the arts and the sciences, agricultural system
that made use of extensive systems of irrigation, created a
surplus, became wealthy, then servile to priests

D. had first codes of law, extensive writing, schools and libraries, use of gold and silver as money, foundations of grammar,
mathematics, medicine, astronomy, and philosophy

E. systems of business and education, techniques of mining
and engineering, foundations of calculus and trigonometry,
advances in medicine, chemistry, astronomy, and physics

Glance back up at those just one more time. Logically, they
seem to follow each other fairly well, don't they? But that wasn't
the way things happened at all! (The above capsule descriptions
represent (A) the Middle Ages, (B) Rome, (C) Egypt, (D) Mesopotamia, and (E) Greece. That's the "logical" order of civilizations
that we asked you to put in "chronological" order.)

Chronological order *makes* sense, but only a *narrow* sense. Let's
say your ex-boyfriend is visiting you in New York, and you mis-
place him somewhere in midtown, so you begin to retrace your
steps. You go back past the hot-dog stand in Central Park, past
the horses and carriages, back down Fifth Avenue, and up to the
top of the Empire State Building, where you find him attempting
to swat down planes.

Did you head back logically or chronologically? The answer is
"both." The chronological order is a feeble force compared to
logical order.

Here are more exercises continuing the same timeline:

**THE RENAISSANCE (1300–1650) began in Italy after the opening of
trade routes made the nation wealthy again. The Italians, who had long
missed their classical world, now had enough money to produce a "re-
birth" of it. They generated great rivalries in cultural patronage, producing a soaring of excellence in architecture, painting, and scholarship
in general. Elsewhere in Europe, countries were changing from feudalism
to capitalism, Martin Luther began the Reformation, Columbus discovered**

the New World, Copernicus and Galileo described a new universe, and England soon had its own Renaissance.

THE AGE OF REASON (1650–1800) describes the period in France and in much of Europe during which religious doctrine was replaced by an enthusiasm for learning. In earlier years, the growth of knowledge had been hindered by superstition, censorship, and control of education, but philosophy and science eventually prevailed, and great advances were made in mathematics, chemistry, physics, astronomy, and more.

THE FRENCH REVOLUTION (1789–1795) brought to an end the old social order in France, which had been composed of an aristocratic class, a feudal peasant class, a comfortable urban middle class, and a very poor urban class of people. This last group rioted, and they were soon joined by the peasants. Both groups were urged on by the middle classes, who had taken a dislike to the nobility and wanted to rule the government themselves. Events mushroomed rapidly out of control, and the urban poor and peasants took it upon themselves to execute the king, the queen, and the rest of the aristocrats, marking the death of feudalism and the arrival of capitalism.

THE AGE OF NAPOLEON (1795–1815) grew out of the French Revolution. Napoleon Bonaparte called himself a healer, although he was a dictatorial one, because he didn't believe that the masses were competent to govern themselves. Proving that he had even greater aspirations, he crowned himself emperor and managed to conquer more than half of Europe. Eventually, an alliance of Russia, Great Britain, Austria, and Prussia took Paris, exiling Napoleon to the island of Elba, from where he escaped and was defeated for the last time at Waterloo.

THE INDUSTRIAL REVOLUTION (1800–1900) is the term used for the transition from an agricultural and craftwork economy to one characterized by industry and machine production. This transition led to rapid economic growth through greatly increased productivity, while improved methods of transportation such as the railroad were able to ship goods far more efficiently than ever before. The rise of factories also led to new social theories, such as socialism itself, which was later refined into doctrine by Karl Marx. The first workers' party was founded in Germany, where widely varying socialist theories would eventually erupt in a flaming Holocaust.

Here are the names of those five eras again. Just put them in chronological order; they defy any other kind of logic:

(A) the Renaissance, (B) the Age of Reason, (C) the Age of Napoleon, (D) the French Revolution, and (E) the Industrial Revolution

---

Illogical as chronological order can be, it still makes its own peculiar kind of sense. If you're a Beatles fan, you've probably nearly memorized the *Sgt. Pepper's Lonely Hearts Club Band* album, except for the portions where the producer recorded a segment, say, a pipe organ solo, then cut it into pieces, mixed them up, and randomly spliced them all back together again—weird for the sake of being weird. And then there's Kurt Vonnegut's *Slaughterhouse 5*, in which a man experiences the events of his life in random order. Or how about Martin Amis' book called *Time's Arrow*, in which the story is told in reverse chronological order? The characters get younger, babies slip back inside their mothers, and people leave their doctors feeling worse instead of better. Ah, time. To the thing itself, and how we spend it, the following passage pertains:

> The great wish of some is to avenge themselves on some particular enemy, the great wish of others to save their own pocket. Slow in assembling, they devote a very small fraction of time to the consideration of any public object, most of it to the prosecution of their own objects. Meanwhile each fancies that no harm will come of his neglect, that it is the business of somebody else to look after this or that for him; and so, by the same notion being entertained by all separately, the common cause imperceptibly decays.

It was written in the fifth century B.C. by Thucydides in his *History of the Peloponnesian War*, but it could have been written by any man in any time throughout history. Such is how little times change, no matter how much times change.

Part Four

ABSTRACT THINKING

BOOK THIRTEEN

Spatial Ability
Three Dimensions

How well can you visualize three-dimensional objects in space?

1. If I'm listening to a description of an object, I don't usually bother to actually envision it. I just listen.
2. And if I do, it's in two dimensions, not three.
3. I don't have much problem with three dimensions. In fact, I can see images almost like a snapshot.
4. Three-dimensional objects aren't too bad, as long as they're just sitting there. But if you ask me to rotate them, I could short out an EEG machine.
5. I don't need to think in three dimensions. After all, I'm not an architect. Or an engineer. Or a mathematician. Or a chemist. Or a physicist. Or a sculptor. Or a painter. Or—

Answers of "true" to number 1 and number 2 are normal. So is a "true" to number 3, but snapshots are *two*-dimensional, not three. A "true" to number 4 is normal, too, but getting better. The attitude expressed in number 5 is also common. But the list of people who need to think in three dimensions is longer than you would have thought, isn't it?! And it only reflects a small part of the world that would open up if you became more comfortable in three dimensions.

Here are some exercises, taken from the subject of solid geometry:

The following compose a class of three-dimensional geometric shapes known to the Greeks as the five regular polyhedra. First look at the three different views of the same shape, then determine which object it was from those illustrated below.

1. Here are three views of one of the regular polyhedra:

 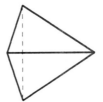 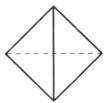

Which of the following is another view of the above object?

A

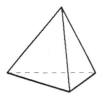

Tetrahedron

B

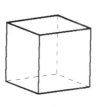

Cube

C

Octahedron

2. Here are three views of another of the regular polyhedra:

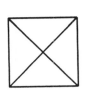  

Which of the following is another view of the above object?

A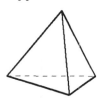

B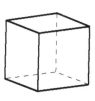

C

Tetrahedron

Cube

Octahedron

3. Here are three views of another of the regular polyhedra:

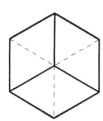 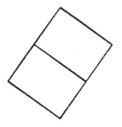 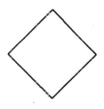

Which of the following is another view of the above object?

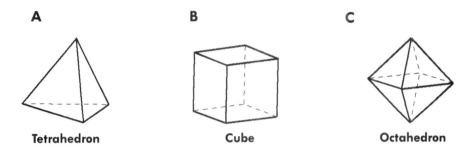

A

Tetrahedron

B

Cube

C

Octahedron

And here are the answers: (1) A, (2) C, and (3) B.

How did you do? They were tricky, weren't they? You might try making these three shapes yourself and rotating them to see how different they can look from unusual oblique angles. (That soft, almost compressible green floral foam that you can buy at many florists works very well and cuts easily with a table knife.)

Three-Dimensional Spatial Ability

If you have difficulty "picturing" three-dimensional objects—and even if you don't—try closing your eyes while you do it. It can be extraordinarily difficult with the usual visual distraction, and even an unadorned wall provides too much. But don't expect to "draw" the objects in the darkness; that is, don't use your eyes at all. Instead, close your eyes and picture them in your "mind's eye," but as clear glass.

Here's a trick I use myself. When I've got the object in mind, I don't try to rotate it. Instead, I let it just sit there on an invisible table, and I "walk" very slowly around to look at it from another angle. Go ahead; try it with a cube that has a dot on one face.

The ability to visualize objects in space is an important part of the learning process, and people who can more readily translate spoken or written instructions into real-life situations are more successful at accomplishing a given task.

Even the more mundane chores in life are made easier by this ability. For example, when was the last time you consulted an instruction manual or sheet with illustrations that looked like they were drawn by a budding Jan Vermeer? Not recently, we'll bet. Instead, you were probably presented with insets of odd-looking parts and assembled fragments and arrows and little numbers and letters. Just the *memory* of assembling that first swing set is enough to cause many a parent to awaken in the middle of the night in a cold sweat.

Here are more exercises, to be done the same way:

4. Here are three views of one of the regular polyhedra:

Which of the following is another view of the above object?

A   **B**   **C**

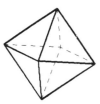

Octahedron   Dodecahedron   Icosahedron

5. Here are three views of one of the regular polyhedra:

Which of the following is another view of the above object?

A

Octahedron

B

Dodecahedron

C

Icosahedron

And here are the answers: (4) C, and (5) C. (Okay, so we tricked you.)

And how about these?

6. Here are three views of one of the regular polyhedra:

Which of the following is another view of the above object?

A

Octahedron

B

Dodecahedron

C

Icosahedron

7. Here are three views of one of the regular polyhedra:

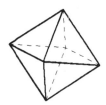

Which of the following is another view of the above object?

A

Octahedron

B

Dodecahedron

C

Icosahedron

And here are the answers: (6) B, and (7) B. (Don't blame us for trying, will you?)

An increased ability to handle spatial relationships, among the most difficult intellectual tasks, may even have another added benefit. And this is not meant to be a metaphor; instead, it's a theory. We all know how difficult it is to "see ourselves as others see us" or "see the other person's point of view." Oh, we *think* we do it, but we really don't. Just consider someone you might meet at a cocktail party—a loud-mouthed, incessant talker, for example. This person probably thinks he's coming across just fine, while you're desperately searching over his shoulder for a familiar face across the room and an excuse to get away from him. But if he *really knew* how odious he was, he might change his behavior. There's a little of that fellow in all of us. (And sometimes more than a little.)

I'm reminded of the times I've given talks for businesses and universities that were videotaped. Looking at the tapes afterward has been a real eye-opener. Likewise for television appearances. I've seen things about myself that I never saw beforehand. And I've been able to change—although it hasn't been easy.

My theory is that an ability to accurately "see" objects, people, and issues from different perspectives may be a related, pervasive trait, and one that can be learned. Considering the influence of the "Ask Marilyn" column I write for *Parade,* I've felt a great responsibility to possess this ability, and I've had considerable success strengthening it. Plenty of mental energy has been expended, but the results have been worth far more than the time I've spent.

Spatial Ability
Four Dimensions

How well can you envision an object that changes over time?

1. I'm appalled when I see people again for the first time in years. They've changed so drastically, and *I* haven't changed so much!
2. "Before" and "after" diet photographs are usually mind-boggling to me. I see why advertisers use them.
3. Instruction booklets that show already-assembled objects instead of assembly-in-progress are nearly impossible for me to follow.
4. I can become totally absorbed watching time-lapse photography in nature shows.
5. Every time I watch *Poltergeist* on the late show, I get very good at imagining the movement of stationary objects. Sometimes I even see shadowy figures lurking around my house. Wait . . . I don't remember leaving that glass on the piano . . .

Answers of "True" to number 1 and number 2 are perfectly normal and probably just the result of a little garden-variety wishful thinking. A "true" to number 3 is common, too, but shows you could strengthen this area. Time-lapse photography is a personal favorite of mine, so I'm biased toward a "true" for number 4. (But isn't everyone?!) And a "true" to number 5? Hmm. It sounds like you've got something much worse than ghosts—you've got *guests!*

Let's begin with some exercises.

Do you remember the three-dimensional geometric shapes known as the five regular polyhedra? They'll appear again in the coming pages, but changed over "time," which we (and many others) call the "fourth dimension." In this section, each side of one three-dimensional figure will be numbered. Beneath it, that same three-dimensional figure will be "unfolded" to form a two-dimensional figure. As rapidly as possible, your task is to tell which segments are which, using the letters marking the segments.

1. Here's the tetrahedron in three dimensions:

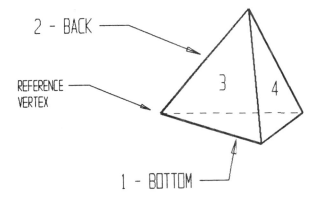

And here's the same tetrahedron unfolded (A=1):

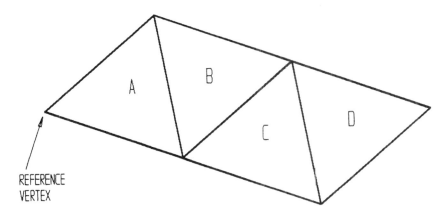

Here are the answers: (1) A, (2) C, (3) D, and (4) B.

2. Here's the cube in three dimensions:

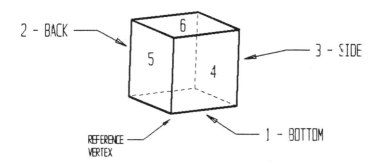

And here's the same cube unfolded (A=1):

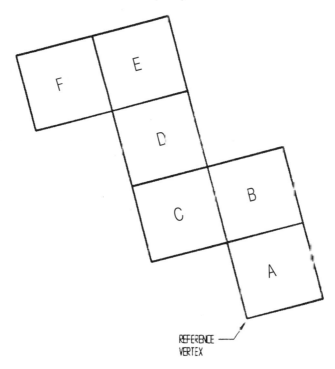

Here are the answers: (1) A, (2) E, (3) B, (4) C, (5) F, and (6) D.

3. Here's the octahedron in three dimensions:

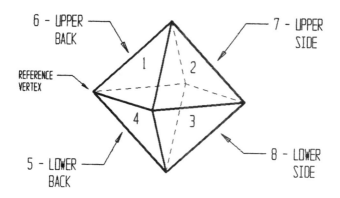

And here's the same octahedron unfolded (A=1):

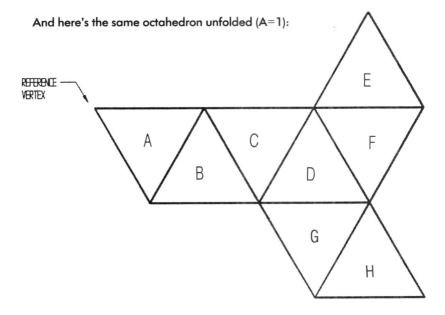

Here are the answers: (1) A, (2) B, (3) G, (4) H, (5) F, (6) E, (7) C, and (8) D.

Four-Dimensional Spatial Ability

Those were quite a bit harder than you would have thought, weren't they? Somehow, it seems as though labeling the sides of a cube would be a snap, and you probably got that one correct with time, but thinking it through was still something like trying to walk fast underwater, wasn't it? (Then again, if you're good at origami, you may have found these very easy, and you're one up on me. I spent *hours* trying to make that darn dolphin!)

But you can be happy we used time as the fourth dimension, instead of presenting you with a "tesseract" (also known as a "hypercube"), the "four-dimensional" analogue of a cube, as shown (theoretically, of course) below:

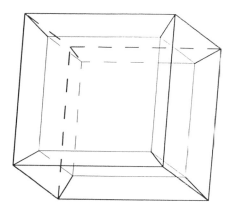

I jokingly implied that fans of origami (oh-rih-GAH-mee) would have an advantage in this section, and that's true. (For those unfamiliar with this charming Japanese craftwork, "origami" is the art of folding paper into shapes, such as flowers or birds; anyone who has ever thrown a paper airplane in school has practiced origami.) So it makes sense that a good way to exercise and improve your spatial ability is buy a book on origami and see how to transform a flat sheet of paper into a swan, for example. Some objects are easy, some are a challenge, and all are certainly fun—not to mention a relatively inexpensive form of entertainment and education. Try it sometime with a neighbor's child and watch his or her excitement grow along with your paper garden.

Actually, many kinds of hands-on work are good for improving your spatial abilities, which is one reason why the bookworm suffers, living in a self-imposed "Flatland," as he or she sometimes does. Books are necessary, of course, but they're not the only road to education, and if they're used to the exclusion of all else, the reader is *less* fit, not more—not just mentally, but also physically, of course. Activity is the key. Build things. Take things apart. Move things around. Don't throw away that old clock or telephone. Put it in a closet, wait for a rainy day, and take it apart first. (Do what you always wanted to do as a kid!) Then try to put it back together again. And *then* throw it away. Learning *can* be a lot of fun!

Now, let's continue with more exercises:

If you've been fearful about this next section, knowing that the dodecahedron and icosahedron lie ahead, rest assured. You're right! But they're so awful that we want you to try them for extra credit only. And because they're so awful, all you're going to have to do is determine which of the unfolded choices could be folded back into the correct shape. (You've got our permission to skip these two pages!)

4. Here's the dodecahedron in three dimensions:

And here are three unfoldings. Which one(s) could be refolded into a dodecahedron?

(A)

(B)

(C)

Here is the answer: (4) A and C could be refolded into dodecahedrons.

5. Here's the icosahedron in three dimensions:

And here are three unfoldings. Which one(s) could be refolded into an icosahedron?

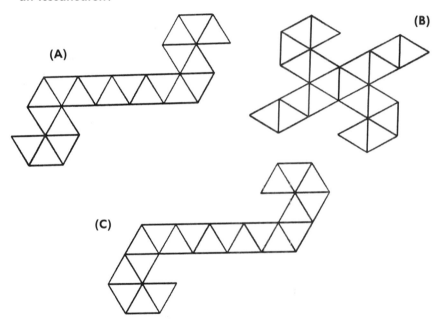

(A)

(B)

(C)

Here is the answer: (5) A, B, and C could all be refolded into icosahedrons.

My research assistant, Richard, relates this true story. When he was in the fourth grade (what a memory!), he had a run-in with a teacher with good spatial ability. Once, when she was out of the classroom, he took the opportunity to hurriedly construct a paper airplane from his math worksheet. His arm was poised in mid-throw when the teacher walked back into the room unexpectedly.

Quickly, he unfolded the airplane, smoothed it out, and pretended to be studying the math problem on it. But the teacher was no fool. She strode purposefully across the room and stood looming over his desk. Grabbing the paper, she studied the folds and asked what was going on. My (aspiring) assistant fumbled for some kind of response and made up something that was only slightly believable. (He tells me that he has always felt a sort of moral obligation not to tell lies that are entirely believable, so his usually involved some kind of aliens.) But because his teacher was able to follow the folds and reconstruct the plane (what spatial ability!), thus disproving the existence of the aliens, he was sentenced to spend half an hour after school writing the sentence "I shouldn't throw paper airplanes" over and over on the blackboard.

But he was more clever than she was in the long run. The boy had foresightedly taught himself how to write with chalk so that it screeched again and again, and although his teacher had too much pride to admit defeat, that half-hour was over after only fifteen minutes.

BOOK FOURTEEN

Orientation

On a Local Scale

How good is your orientation on a local scale?

1. You wouldn't believe how much time I've spent wandering through parking lots in search of my car.
2. I become anxious when I'm in unknown territory.
3. When I'm in an unfamiliar area, I often have to ask for directions.
4. Well, *I* never need to ask for directions!
5. None of this is much of a problem for me as long as I have a map. But without a map, I look a lot like a lost dog.

"True" to number 1? Oh, that's normal, for heaven's sake; don't worry about it. And it must be particularly common among the French; the last time I paid them a visit, about ninety percent of them were driving Renaults, and about ninety percent of the Renaults were either blue or gray. It must drive them nuts! Answer of "true" to number 2? It's very common, but it's a big handicap in life, too. You should make a great effort to conquer this mild agoraphobia. "True" to number 3? You're a woman, right? "True" to number 4? You're a man, right? And "true" to number 5? Why, you sound just like *me!*

Here are some exercises that use the geography of the United States. Study each map for at least a minute, then pretend you're campaigning for the presidency, cover the map with your hand, and answer the questions beneath it.

1. These are the New England states:

(A) After many fruitless years in Congress, you manage to get a piece of original legislation passed. Exhilarated, you declare your candidacy for President in Rhode Island, then travel one state to the west. What state are you in now?

(B) A cagey radical group questions you about your bill—earthworm relief that would make wet sidewalks safer. Does it protect the worms themselves or just squeamish people? You leave hurriedly and travel one state north. To what state?

(C) You put on last year's Armani suit and declare yourself to be the champion of the average man before taking your campaign one state north to Vermont, then east through New Hampshire. What state are you in now?

2. These are the Mid-Atlantic states:

(A) You fly to western upstate New York, then travel two states south before you hear that your running mate's wife has been lobbying to have certain species of fish declared obscene. You go back north one state to talk to her. To what state?

(B) A part-time pretzel-bender in Delaware claims that she had a torrid affair with you ten years ago and is trying to meet up with your campaign. She travels northeast through New Jersey, then due north one state. What state is she in?

(C) The next day, an unemployed live-bait salesman claims that *he* had an affair with you only *five* years ago, and he and the pretzel-bender start a tabloid war. You pass through eastern Maryland and stop one state to the south. Where are you?

3. These are the Southeast states:

(A) You fly to Mississippi and try to look local by changing to last year's Dior suit, but it's too late in the season for white, so you head east through Alabama and Georgia, then through South Carolina to the state just to the north. What one is it?

(B) Charges are made that you tried to avoid the draft in the 1960's. Indignant, you explain that your apartment was not well-insulated, and you were only trying to avoid *catching* a draft. In a huff, you travel as far south as you can. To what state?

(C) Touring an assembly line, you press a shiny blue button. Amid the resulting roar of machinery, a reporter becomes part of the exhaust system of a luxury sedan. You head one state north, two states west, and one state southwest. Where are you now?

Here are the answers: 1. (A) Connecticut, (B) Massachusetts, and (C) Maine. 2. (A) Pennsylvania, (B) New York, and (C) Virginia. 3. (A) North Carolina, (B) Florida (Key West, actually), and (C) Louisiana.

Orientation on a Local Scale

A lack of a sense of orientation is very, very common, but it is especially easy to correct. First, get into the driver's seat, and we mean that literally. If you feel that your sense of direction is weak—whether around town or when you're driving to another state on vacation—we're willing to bet that you're usually the passenger, at least on the unfamiliar trips. Women in particular are prone to this sort of passivity. Oh, they drive themselves and chauffeur others around town plenty often, maybe even most of the time overall, but when it comes to going anywhere different—whether it's a new restaurant on the other side of town or a sight-seeing vacation through the Rockies—they let the man drive. This one habit alone is utterly devastating for a woman's sense of direction. Not recognizing this, women continue to let the men drive them, not necessarily to the grocery store, but usually to the seashore, because "he's just better at this than I am," thereby aggravating the difference endlessly, eventually making the two seem worlds apart.

Remember the last time you flew to a strange city, and a friend or relative picked you up and drove you around in his or her car throughout your stay there? You couldn't have found any of those places again on your own, could you? And if it hadn't been for the sun, you wouldn't have known whether you were heading north or south, right? The passenger remains in a fog. But when you have to rent a car at the airport and drive yourself to those same places instead, you learn the directions as soon as you go there just once, and you'll know whether the airport was to the east or west of the city and whether your hotel was north or south of it.

Try it, and don't give up. Unless you're agoraphobic, the most persistent case of lack of orientation will crack under this method. (And it may even help alleviate the symptoms of the mildly agoraphobic individual.) But don't allow yourself simply to be the robot arms of whoever may be wielding the map. Instead, take the map yourself and stop the car whenever you need to read it.

And speaking of maps, here's a way you can improve your sense of direction right at home. First, take your desk and face it due north. (This may be a bit of a pain, but you don't have to leave it that way forever.) Second, get a big, rectangular, topographical map of the United States, but one with as little clutter as possible. The best would have the states strongly outlined and labeled so you can read their names at a glance. Finally, affix it to the top of your desk, right over the work surface, where you can see it beneath you each time you work. After a few months, replace it with a map of your state and its neighbors, and eventually replace that with a map of your city and its environs.

Back to the exercises.

4. These are Midwest states:

(A) Landing in Ohio, you're met by an angry group holding an "F.O.E." banner; they're members of the new organization called "Friends of Earthworms." You escape to travel west through Indiana and on to the state just to the west of it. What state?

(B) The bait salesman claims he also had an affair with your running mate's wife, citing her antifish stance as proof; she denies it, citing a traumatic childhood experience with a guppy. You pass through southern Iowa and stop just to the west. Where?

(C) America's farmers charge that you're out of touch with their concerns when a farmer shows you his prizewinning bull and you attempt to milk it. The bull chases you east one state. What state are you in now?

5. These are the Southwest states:

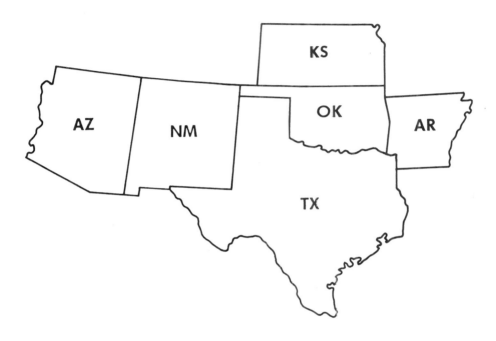

(A) Losing the bull in Arkansas, you sample some fine local moon-shine. The press snaps a picture of you with a gallon jug to your lips, and you maintain that although you tasted it, you didn't swallow. Quietly, you fly west one state. What state is that?

(B) While on the prairies, you reflect on the source of your interest in earthworms and wonder if the bait salesman really *did* have an affair with your running mate's wife. Jealous, you take your campaign one state to the south. To which state?

(C) After envisioning the live-bait salesman and your running mate's wife having drinks together, you run into an old friend and ask *him* to be your running mate instead, but he refuses. You take your campaign west through New Mexico and into what state?

6. These are the Plains and Mountain states:

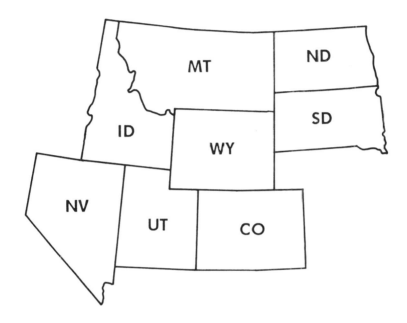

(A) You fly to the convention in southern South Dakota and win the nomination despite heckling by the radical group of marine biologists "Vote for Vertebrates," who call you spineless. Beaming, you take your campaign one state due west. To where?

(B) The pretzel-bender is still on your trail. She sends you a telegram from Nevada calling you "a worm" and saying that she is traveling east into Utah, then north through Idaho and into the state to the north of it. Where has she ended up?

(C) You send her a telegram replying, "Thank you," and while she heads north, you head south. After hearing that your running mate's wife had a nervous breakdown at Sea World, you travel south into Utah and then one state to the east. Where are you?

7. These are the Pacific states:

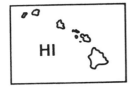

(A) You land in California to find animal-rights activists protesting both for and against your "earthworm" legislation. Now you know the downside of equivocation. You get back onto the plane and fly one state to the west. What state is that?

(B) You fly one state to the east, then drive your new luxury sedan through Oregon. Your wife hears voices coming from the exhaust system, and you stop in the next state to the north. What state is it?

(C) The campaign is over. After a comparatively relaxing break during which you watch a videotape of volcanic eruptions, you fly northwest, over Canada, to the first state you come to. In which state do you watch the election returns?

And here are the answers: 4. (A) Illinois, (B) Nebraska, and (C) Iowa. 5. (A) Oklahoma, (B) Texas, and (C) Arizona. 6. (A) Wyoming, (B) Montana, and (C) Colorado. 7. (A) Hawaii, (B) Washington, and (C) Alaska.

But we couldn't end this section without addressing that popular question, "Why don't men want to ask for directions?" Just recently, a study was performed in which men and women were asked to find their way through ratlike mazes, and it was discovered that the two sexes navigated very differently. The men relied on vectors, using estimates of direction, speed, and time to construct a "mental map." Women, however, relied on landmarks. For this reason, the researchers concluded that men don't ask for directions because they don't feel lost; they feel their "intuitive" maps will get them where they want to go eventually. But the researchers also found that neither the male nor the female methodology was more efficient. This seems to call their conclusion into question. In other words, if men and women are equally proficient, why is it only the men who "don't feel lost"?

Here's a possibility. After spending most of their lives in charge of their own navigation, men know intuitively that asking for directions interferes with the learning process. That is, they know they're better off if they find the way themselves.

So the next time you're standing on a Manhattan street corner and someone asks you, "How do you get to Carnegie Hall?," do them a favor and answer, "Practice."

Orientation

And on a Global One

How good is your orientation on a global scale?

1. I was scarred as a child when my parents bought me a very cheap globe. It was shaped like a pyramid. I've been bad with geography ever since. (But I do see Egypt as a world power.)
2. Honestly, I think I'm just hopeless in this whole subject. I've forgotten everything I learned in school! And the names of the countries keep changing, anyway.
3. Oddly, I can pinpoint Iraq on a map, but not New Jersey.
4. Let's see, latitude goes north-south and describes points east-west . . . no, longitude goes east-west and describes points north-south . . . no, latitude goes—oh, shoot!
5. When I studied psychology in school, I thought that longitudinal studies were all conducted on the prime meridian.

Okay, so number 1 was a bad joke, but a "true" to number 2 is normal, even if not exactly desirable. So is a "true" to number 3; Iraq was the subject of much news coverage, but you probably left the geography of the United States back in high school. A "true" to number 4 is normal, too, for the same reason. And yes, number 5 was another bad joke. We're not perfect, you know.

Here are exercises that use the geography of the world:

Let's pretend you're part of a group taking a "Countries in the News" world tour.

1. This is Europe:

(A) Beginning in England, a tourist harasses a palace guard; she is found stuffed into the guard's big furry hat. Debating whether she should continue with the passengers or the luggage, your group flies on to Hungary, then drives one country south. Where are you?

(B) In Sarajevo, you all stand and watch Bobby Fischer lobbing grenades into a building, crying, "Checkmate, you fool!" then head northwest to Austria, northeast through Czechoslovakia, then north one country. What country are you in now?

(C) In Poland, the home of Solidarity, you sign a petition for its vanquished rival, the Liquidarity Party, which only asks politely that workers be given afternoon juice breaks. You head east into Belarus, then east one more country. To which country?

2. This is Asia:

(A) At a Moscow hotel, a tour member is overheard singing "Georgia on My Mind" in the shower, and a KGB agent arrests him on suspicion of supplying arms to the republics. You then head south into Mongolia, then south one more country. To where?

(B) At Tiananmen Square, times have changed; all you find is a lone student trying to keep an overweight Party member from reaching an eclair. You travel southwest through Nepal, India, and Pakistan, stopping one country to the northwest. Which one?

(C) The tourist is finally extricated from the big furry hat, but her camera is firmly embedded in her forehead. However, she does manage to land the lead in a revival of *I Am a Camera*. You all travel one country west. Which country are you in now?

3. This is Africa and the Middle East:

(A) **After walking from Iran to Iraq, the comment, "I'm dead on my feet," is taken as an invitation. However, your bus driver is a former New York cabbie, so avoiding a missile attack isn't a problem. You arrive in the country due south. Which one is it?**

(B) **In Libya, the CIA wires you for sound. You buy a snow cone and sit by terrorists planning to hide explosives in soap-on-a-rope, but your slurping muffles their voices. You travel south through Sudan, then due east two countries. To where?**

(C) **You drive to Kenya, where you receive a surprise gift; as you pull out a soap-on-a-rope, the bus hits a pothole, and it clatters to the floor. The resulting blast blows you as far south in Africa as you can go. What country do you rain down on?**

Here are the answers: 1. (A) France, (B) Poland, and (C) Russia. 2. (A) China, (B) Afghanistan, and (C) Iran. 3. (A) Saudi Arabia, (B) Somalia, and (C) South Africa.

Orientation on a Global Scale

What? You don't own a globe? That's as bad as not owning an atlas! And owning an atlas alone isn't good enough. (Remember what happens when you spread out the surface of a sphere onto a plane surface.) So the first thing to do is to buy yourself the biggest possible, most accurate globe you can find, preferably one that has a modest amount of topography indicated, but few, if any, cities. Best is a globe with countries that are clearly outlined in different colors. (Some people like the new transparent globes, but it's up to you. Don't, however, buy one just because it's different or for decorating purposes.)

Save it for a rainy Sunday afternoon, then make yourself a cup of coffee or tea, take the globe out of the box, and explore it. Then, after you've spent a little time with it, go get the front page from your Sunday paper, take any foreign story at random, and find that place on the globe. But *don't* look it up by its map coordinates; you won't learn enough that way. Instead, go to the continent in question and simply search for it yourself. Do the same with another story, then another. After a month (or two) of Sundays, you'll find yourself with the best news-based knowledge of the globe that you've ever had and maybe even a new-found enthusiasm for it all.

Now it's time to plan a dream vacation—six months of travel around the world. (Maybe you'll win a lottery, or maybe you'll retire and decide to spend some of the money that you were going to leave the kids, who would probably have taken your dream vacation *for* you; you can relieve them of this burden.)

On another rainy weekend, first list a dozen exotic destination countries. Then spend some time looking over your globe very carefully to discover if there are any more locations that you may have forgotten. (You have six months to travel, remember!) Be sure to explore all the landmasses thoroughly, but don't forget to check the oceans, or your fingers will walk right over Easter Island.

Then, starting in your home state, plot a route to fly directly to the closest destination. But *is* it the closest one? Use a piece of string to find out. And are you going by the shortest route? Maybe it's shorter to fly over the pole. Check. Or maybe it's shorter to fly east around the world instead of west (or vice versa). Then, after you've checked all that out for your first destination, do the same with the next-closest destination. You're not sure which that is? Use the string to find out. Continue this way until you've planned your entire vacation route.

And for an extra boost to your learning experience, note the number of miles you travel between each destination, comparing it to a cross-country (New York–Los Angeles) flight here in your own country. This is easily calculated by measuring the string according to the scale on the globe (say, 1 inch equals 500 miles).

Back to more exercises (following your convalescence in Greenland).

4. This is North America:

(A) In Greenland, you wonder if you're gaining weight on this vacation when a nearsighted native mistakes you for a walrus and attempts to remove your tusks. You flee across the ice, sliding one country to the southwest. Which country are you in now?

(B) You rejoin the repaired bus in Canada, where the tour director fits you with braces at no charge if you promise not to open any more surprise gifts. You head through the U.S.A. down to Florida, then sail one country south. Which country is it?

(C) A tour member is mistaken for Fidel Castro and kidnapped. The Cuban government receives a ransom demand, but no one wants him back. The kidnappers have several half-price sales and finally return the kidnappee to the bus. You then sail due west. To where?

5. This is South America:

(A) In Guyana, the tour visits the recently opened Jim Jones theme park; you are happy to find that there is no line at the refreshment stand. You travel one country to the south. What country is it?

(B) You head south to Bolivia, dining in a bistro called Chez Guevara. In Argentina, a British tourist accuses you of swiping her souvenir Leopoldo Galtieri action figure; you say you've never even heard of him, then travel one country west. To where?

(C) You head north through Peru and into Ecuador where the tour member wearing the big furry hat is taken for a messiah and carried off by the natives. You trade them her Leopoldo Galtieri action figure for her, then flee north one country. To where?

6. This is Australia, the Pacific, and Antarctica:

(A) Succumbing to jet lag in Australia, some members of the tour group begin to think they're marsupials, and the hotel gift shop runs clean out of extra-large baggies. In the morning, you travel east to the first set of islands. What country is it?

(B) You fly northwest to a hotel in the Philippines, where you're handed a complimentary soap-on-a-rope and faint. You're carried onto the plane, and the tour group flies as far south as they can possibly go. Where is everyone now?

(C) You mush across the Ross Ice Shelf and reach the South Pole, where the dogs insist that they actually got to the pole before you did. The next morning, you all fly to Hawaii, then head east, stopping in the first country you see. Where are you?

And here are the answers: 4. (A) Canada, (B) Cuba, and (C) Mexico. 5. (A) Brazil, (B) Chile, and (C) Colombia. 6. (A) New Zealand, (B) Antarctica, and (C) the United States (home!).

Global coordinates are useful, of course, but more as aids to identification and navigation than to orientation. The latitude lines are called "parallels" because they run parallel to each other around the globe from east to west. They describe points north and south. Longitude lines run north and south but are not parallels; instead, they meet at the poles and radiate outward. They describe points east and west of the prime meridian at Greenwich, England. The two sets of lines on a globe (or map) form a graph, on which can be plotted a point that describes any particular location. For example, we are now sitting at 40°45' north latitude and 74° west longitude; with further division, we can demonstrate even more accuracy.

But orientation skills are less like map skills than they are like visualization skills. However, instead of developing the ability to visualize stationary and moving objects alone, orientation requires that you put yourself into the picture.

Maybe it's partly biological; for example, bacteria and bees have magnetite within their bodies that allows them to use the earth's magnetic field to orient themselves. And pigeons, no stranger to "homing" instincts, have magnetite structures in their brains. Who knows what wonders humans might possess?

BOOK FIFTEEN

Design and Assembly

Speed

How fast can you assemble things?

1. I find it difficult to put my thoughts together to form a well-organized essay; when registering for a course, the first thing I check is whether I am required to write a thesis. And then I register for something else. Anything.
2. I'm not bad at assembling objects, really, but I always seem to have parts left over when I'm finished.
3. I'm okay—as long as I can take as much time as I like; time pressure really ruins my concentration.
4. I'm okay—as long as I have a deadline; if I'm not under time pressure, I take forever to make a decision.
5. I do pretty well, because I've gotten used to relying on the inherent logic of the structure rather than on my memory or someone else's outline or instructions.

A "true" to number 1, number 2, number 3, and number 4 is very normal, even if that's not the way we'd *prefer* to be. But simple practice can eliminate much of the discomfort we feel when we need to assemble something. A "true" to number 5 is unusual, but excellent. You can skip this chapter. Unless you'd like to read some of the most beautiful poetry ever written. Hmm?

Here are some exercises. First read the lines carefully; then without looking back, reassemble the same poem from the disassembled lines beneath it. (Try timing yourself here.)

1. WILLIAM SHAKESPEARE: from "Sonnet 18"

Shall I compare thee to a summer's day?
Thou art more lovely and more temperate:
Rough winds do shake the darling buds of May,
And summer's lease hath all too short a date:

Assemble the excerpt from the following lines:
(A) Rough winds do shake the darling buds of May
(B) Thou art more lovely and more temperate
(C) And summer's lease hath all too short a date
(D) Shall I compare thee to a summer's day

2. JOHN DONNE: from "Sonnet 10" (*Holy Sonnets*)

Death, be not proud, though some have called thee
Mighty and dreadful, for thou art not so;
For those whom thou think'st thou dost overthrow
Die not, poor Death, nor yet canst thou kill me.

Assemble the excerpt from the following lines:
(A) Die not, poor Death, not yet canst thou kill me
(B) Mighty and dreadful, for thou art not so
(C) Death, be not proud, though some have called thee
(D) For those whom thou think'st thou dost overthrow

3. JOHN MILTON: from *Paradise Lost*

What in me is dark
Illumine; what is low, raise and support;
That, to the height of this great argument,
I may assert Eternal Providence,
And justify the ways of God to men.

Assemble the excerpt from the following lines:
(A) I may assert Eternal Providence

(B) What in me is dark
(C) That, to the height of this great argument
(D) Illumine; what is low, raise and support
(E) And justify the ways of God to men

4. ALEXANDER POPE: from *Essay on Man*

Hope springs eternal in the human breast:
Man never is, but always to be blest;
The soul, uneasy and confined from home,
Rests and expatiates in a life to come.

Assemble the excerpt from the following lines:
(A) The soul, uneasy and confined from home,
(B) Man never is, but always to be blest
(C) Hope springs eternal in the human breast
(D) Rests and expatiates in a life to come

Here are the answers: (1) D, B, A, C, (2) C, B, D, A, (3) B, D, C, A, E, and (4) C, B, A, D.

Speed

We removed the punctuation from the disassembled lines so it wouldn't distract you by being too much of a hint; tricks and memory techniques weren't the point here, of course. If they were, you simply could have used a mnemonic device such as noting the first letter of each line . . . STRA in the case of the Shakespeare sonnet. And if you did that, you may have exposed the weakness in relying on devices as a substitute for making the effort to develop real skill. Yes, speed counts here, but we won't give you a time against which to measure yourself. Instead, you should measure the time you need for the first exercise, use *that* as a baseline, and then attempt to improve upon it.

But doesn't "speed kill"? Shouldn't accuracy be more important than speed? Sometimes. But not always. In the moments before a traffic accident, for example, *both* count. And if you can't think fast, you may not be doing any more thinking at all.

The French psychoanalyst Jacques Lacan had the unnerving habit of interrupting a patient's session with the statement, "Okay, that does it, Woody. You've got five minutes. Now, tell me what's important." (We'll admit we paraphrased him just a tiny bit.) Foremost among his reasons was that his "analysands" (patients, to the rest of us) tended to spend their time unconsciously skirting the real issues, only addressing them in the final moments of a session when they knew they were out of time. To avoid this, Lacan imposed a deadline, effectively cutting through the tangle of emotional underbrush.

Why is it that some people thrive on the discipline of the clock while others panic or at least become very uncomfortable by its presence? I don't know, and I don't want to offer you any guesswork. However, I do know that simple practice alleviates the problem, and it's easy to practice. For example, take getting up and going to work or school. Without running or becoming sloppy, could you do it faster? Try. (But only tune up the action that always seems to take "too long." Don't make a pleasurable breakfast an on-the-fly activity.) Unless you're a typical college student and have it honed to the last minute already, cut five minutes from tomorrow's time, adding it to breakfast or to sleep, instead.

Remember, don't just "speed up" your activities in general. Rather, learn to concentrate better on the task at hand. First try a couple of low-mental-energy tasks like the above changes in your morning routine, but then progress to entirely intellectual tasks. Write your next letter a little faster. Read the daily newspaper faster (while still reading the same amount). Do the crossword puzzle faster. Think through your day—at work, at home in the evenings, and on the weekend. You'll find plenty of places to practice.

But the point is not to hurry through life or to save little scraps (or even big chunks) of time here and there. Instead, we want to focus on "figuring things out" faster or "putting things together" faster. And speaking of "putting things together," we've got a few more exercises for you ahead.

The instructions are the same. And do time yourself—at least in order to get the feeling of the clock ticking away while you're working:

   1. **WILLIAM BLAKE: from "Ideas of Good and Evil"**

To see a world in a grain of sand,
And a heaven in a wild flower;
Hold infinity in the palm of your hand,
And eternity in an hour.

Assemble the excerpt from the following lines:
(A) Hold infinity in the palm of your hand
(B) And a heaven in a wild flower
(C) And eternity in an hour
(D) To see a world in a grain of sand

2. WILLIAM WORDSWORTH: from "Lines Written in Early Spring"

To her fair works did Nature link
The human soul that through me ran;
And much it grieved my heart to think
What man has made of man.

Assemble the excerpt from the following lines:
(A) What man has made of man
(B) To her fair works did Nature link
(C) And much it grieved my heart to think
(D) The human soul that through me ran

3. SAMUEL TAYLOR COLERIDGE: from "The Rime of the Ancient Mariner"

Water, water, everywhere,
And all the boards did shrink;
Water, water, everywhere,
Nor any drop to drink.

Assemble the excerpt from the following lines:
(A) Nor any drop to drink
(B) Water, water, everywhere
(C) Water, water, everywhere
(D) And all the boards did shrink

4. George Gordon, Lord Byron: from "She Walks in Beauty"

She walks in beauty, like the night
Of cloudless climes and starry skies;
And all that's best of dark and bright
Meet in her aspect and her eyes;

Assemble the excerpt from the following lines:
(A) Of cloudless climes and starry skies
(B) Meet in her aspect and her eyes
(C) And all that's best of dark and bright
(D) She walks in beauty, like the night

Here are the answers: (1) D, B, A, C, (2) B, D, C, A, (3) B, D, C, A (or C, D, B, A), and (4) D, A, C, B.

Of course, we all want to be able to think more quickly—some of us call it "thinking on our feet"—not to save time, but to get a job accomplished well, from thinking of the right play to call during the closing moments of a football game to the right thing to say during a board meeting.

But the modern world is pressing even more demands upon us. As the rate of technological change in our environment increases exponentially, so does the rate at which jobs need to be done—and that includes all those decisions that need to be made. It wasn't so long ago when life moved at a much more leisurely pace; it wasn't possible to process and transmit information almost instantaneously, even when it would have saved the day. But things like computers and modems and fax machines have changed all that. The problems that plague us now are: (A) What happens when new generations of technology make it necessary to handle work faster than human beings are capable of doing it? (B) What happens when we need to make vital decisions, and there is less and less time to understand the issues that go into making them? and (C) What happens to those people who need to take their time to avoid doing a bad job?

As the modern minute gets shorter and shorter, the need to rapidly "assemble" our thoughts—whether that involves putting together a cogent essay, a compelling argument, or an intelligent decision—becomes more and more important. And if you don't expend the effort to adapt to those changing conditions, you are likely to be replaced by someone who will.

Design and Assembly

Accuracy

How accurately can you assemble things?

1. I am utterly dependent on instruction manuals. I didn't even try to turn on my new car radio without help.
2. Whenever I need to write a report or present an argument, I never seem able to assemble my points as well as the material deserves.
3. I need to have the recipe in front of me—even when I've cooked the same dish half-a-dozen times.
4. I may need a little help at first, but when I've accomplished something once, it's mine.
5. This is my strong point. I actually enjoy putting together those multicolored backyard-jungle gyms.

A "true" to number 1 isn't very worrisome—it just indicates a lack of confidence—but a "true" to number 2 shows that you're suffering from that feeling. A "true" to number 3 again shows a simple lack of confidence. Close the cookbook! How bad could the chicken pot pie possibly turn out?! A "true" to number 4 is probably the ideal goal. But a "true" to number 5? Goodness. What a wonderful neighbor you must make!

Here are some exercises. First read the lines carefully; then read the excerpt below it. Finally, choose the correct final line from the choices given, all written by the same author:

1. JOHN KEATS: from "Ode on a Grecian Urn"

When old age shall this generation waste,
Thou shalt remain, in midst of other woe
Than ours, a friend to man, to whom thou say'st,
"Beauty is truth, truth beauty,"—that is all
Ye know on earth, and all ye need to know.

Here's the excerpt:

When old age shall this generation waste,
Thou shalt remain, in midst of other woe
Than ours, a friend to man, to whom thou say'st,
"Beauty is truth, truth beauty,"—that is all

Which is the correct final line?
(A) And all the bliss to be before tomorrow morn
(B) Ye know on earth, and all ye need to know
(C) Till Love and Fame to nothingness do sink
(D) And so live ever—or else swoon to death

2. PERCY BYSSHE SHELLEY: from "When the Lamp is Shattered"

When the lamp is shattered
The light in the dust lies dead—
When the cloud is scattered
The rainbow's glory is shed.

Here's the excerpt:

When the lamp is shattered
The light in the dust lies dead—
When the cloud is scattered

Which is the correct final line?
(A) I weep for Adonais—he is dead!
(B) The lone and level sands stretch far away

(C) The rainbow's glory is shed
(D) And laugh as I pass in thunder

3. HENRY WADSWORTH LONGFELLOW: from "The Arrow and the Song"

I shot an arrow into the air,
It fell to earth, I knew not where;
For, so swiftly it flew, the sight
Could not follow it in its flight.

Here's the excerpt:

I shot an arrow into the air,
It fell to earth, I knew not where;
For, so swiftly it flew, the sight

Which is the correct final line?
(A) Could not follow it in its flight
(B) A mournful rustling in the dark
(C) Thou, too, sail on, O Ship of State
(D) How far the unknown transcends the what we know

4. EDGAR ALLAN POE: from "The Raven"

Once upon a midnight dreary, while I pondered, weak
    and weary
Over many a quaint and curious volume of forgotten
    lore—
While I nodded, nearly napping, suddenly there came
    a tapping,
As of some one gently rapping, rapping at my chamber
    door.

Here's the excerpt:

Once upon a midnight dreary, while I pondered, weak
    and weary
Over many a quaint and curious volume of forgotten
    lore—
While I nodded, nearly napping, suddenly there came
    a tapping,

Which is the correct final line?
(A) Chilling and killing my Annabel Lee
(B) The summer dream beneath the tamarind tree
(C) On seas less hideously serene
(D) As of someone gently rapping, rapping at my chamber door

And here are the answers: (1) B, (2) C, (3) A, and (4) D.

Accuracy

How did you do? We'll bet you were relieved that you didn't have to race against the clock this time around. Funny, isn't it? Although there was no real pressure in the previous exercise, just the awareness of a clock created the illusion of it.

But now we'll consider another anxiety: depending on yourself. So many of us have gotten so used to following written instructions that we've forgotten how to think on our own. And then we start believing that we actually *can't* think on our own.

Well, you know we're not going to let you get away with believing that, are we? No, it's simply that many of us become accustomed to using crutches here and there, and before we know it, we're out of shape mentally.

When you think of "design and assembly," maybe you think of engineers huddled over drawing boards, busily developing an automobile that runs on electricity or natural gas. Or maybe you think of production lines with robotic arms actually assembling an automobile. Either way, the essence is how things fit together and why—whether it's an automobile or a thought.

A fine way to practice this skill is to diagram sentences a study technique that I personally feel is seriously underrated in both public- and private-school systems. Sentence-diagramming is similar to developing schematics for structural linguistics, and it exercises the very skill we're discussing here in a productive way. The following sentence is diagrammed on the following page: Several angry alligators invaded Bob's editorial office and demanded that they be allowed to write a book about people.

You'll find basic diagramming information in many basic English textbooks.

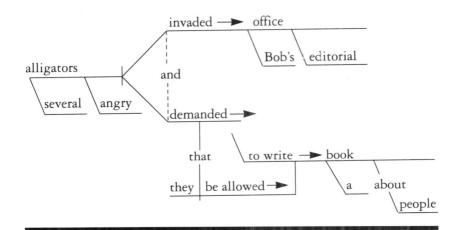

Here are more exercises. The instructions are the same:

1. ALFRED, LORD TENNYSON: from "Locksley Hall"

In the spring a fuller crimson comes upon the
    robin's breast;
In the spring the wanton lapwing gets himself
    another crest;

In the spring a livelier iris changes on the
    burnished dove;
In the spring a young man's fancy lightly turns to
    thoughts of love.

Here's the excerpt:

In the spring a fuller crimson comes upon the
    robin's breast;
In the spring the wanton lapwing gets himself
    another crest;
In the spring a livelier iris changes on the
    burnished dove;

Which is the correct final line?
(A) Beyond the utmost bound of human thought
(B) "I am half sick of shadows," said the Lady of Shalott
(C) In the spring a young man's fancy lightly turns to thoughts of love
(D) And with no language but a cry

2. ROBERT FROST: from "Stopping by Woods on a Snowy Evening"

The woods are lovely, dark and deep
But I have promises to keep,
And miles to go before I sleep,
And miles to go before I sleep.

Here's the excerpt:

The woods are lovely, dark and deep
But I have promises to keep,
And miles to go before I sleep,

Which is the correct final line?
(A) And that has made all the difference
(B) Good fences make good neighbors
(C) With the slow smokeless burning of decay
(D) And miles to go before I sleep

3. WILLIAM BUTLER YEATS: from "Among School Children"

O chestnut-tree, great-rooted blossomer,
Are you the leaf, the blossom or the bole?
O body swayed to music, O brightening glance,
How can we know the dancer from the dance?

Here's the excerpt:

O chestnut-tree, great-rooted blossomer,
Are you the leaf, the blossom or the bole?
O body swayed to music, O brightening glance,

Which is the correct final line?
(A) How can we know the dancer from the dance?
(B) A terrible beauty is born
(C) Of what is past, or passing, or to come
(D) The fury and the mire of human veins

4. T. S. ELIOT: from "The Hollow Men"

This is the way the world ends
This is the way the world ends

This is the way the world ends
Not with a bang but a whimper.

Here's the excerpt:

This is the way the world ends
This is the way the world ends
This is the way the world ends

Which is the correct final line?
(A) April is the cruellest month
(B) Talking of Michelangelo
(C) Not with a bang but a whimper
(D) Birth, copulation and death

And here are the answers: (1) C, (2) D, (3) A, and (4) C.

We've all read about paleontologists who unearth the femur of a long-extinct creature and subsequently manage to determine how tall it might have been and how much it might have weighed. How do they do that? If a femur—a thighbone—is of a particular length and configuration, this may imply the length and configuration of the legs. And this may imply how much weight those legs could have supported. And this may imply other bodily proportions, and so on. With enough scraps of information, scientists can begin to extrapolate (or "design and assemble") what sort of creature it might have been.

The whole history of technology has been the history of putting things together in new and important ways. In the early nineteenth century, people thought "bad air" (known as "miasma")—like the methane exuded by swamps—caused diseases like malaria ("mal'aria" in Italian means "bad air"). In fact, Napoleon himself commissioned a "bad smell" map of Egypt during his campaign there. Accordingly, a freakish "air pistol" was invented that touched off a spark in a gas to see if the air was "bad." And where did *that* lead? Eventually, to automobile spark plugs, among other things.

And so it goes. How did the invention of the plow eventually create civilization? How did civilization create pottery, writing, and money? And how does this book have anything to do with the underwear boom in the fourteenth century?

In the High Middle Ages, after the plague had gone, knickers became all the rage in Europe. Because of the introduction of the spinning wheel and the horizontal loom, the lower classes could now afford linen. And the "bone man," who had collected bones to be ground up for use as fertilizer, soon became the "rag-and-bone man" and now collected worn-out linen. Who had a use for this linen? Paper mills—which were emerging as a rising industry in prosperous times. Compared to parchment, paper was cheap, and there was more of it than anyone knew what to do with. Then a metalworker named Johann Gutenberg invented movable type and later the printing press. Shortly afterward, the publishing industry was born, ultimately bringing enlightenment and education to the masses. And some five hundred years later, a copy of *"I've Forgotten Everything I Learned in School!"* turns up on your bookshelf.

BOOK SIXTEEN

Mental Organization

Speed

How fast are your "mental reflexes"?

1. Sometimes I can't immediately think of my exact age!
2. I often seem to have names or words "on the tip of my tongue" but can't quite get at them.
3. I've had cable television for years, but I still have to consult the conversion chart every time I want to find a channel.
4. For the life of me, I just cannot do math in my head.
5. I'm at my best in a heated argument; when I'm really furious, I can think of regrettable things to say at light speed.

A "true" to number 1 is totally normal; don't worry about it. Once we're past the age of adding "and a half" to it (as in the question, "How old are you, little boy?" and the reply, "Nine and a half!"), the exact number just doesn't matter to us so much anymore. And a "true" to number 2 is normal, too. It's just . . . um . . . oh, what's that word I'm looking for . . . ? But a "true" to number 3? Hide that conversion chart! You need some mental exercise! A "true" to number 4 is common, but it is only partially alleviated by practice; the other part is the result of "math anxiety," a different problem. And a "true" to number 5? Why, you sound just like me!

The exercises in this chapter are all taken from the subject of written music.

Following are some common musical symbols, accompanied by their names and our abbreviations for them in parentheses. Below each group is a blank "exercise grid." Make two or three photocopies of each page so you can complete each grid at least twice.

Here's how to complete the grid: First you'll find a "key" that shows the common symbols we mentioned above. Study it for a few moments. Then, referring to the key as often as you like, place the correct abbreviation below each symbol in the exercise grid, moving from left to right, the way you usually write. (That is, don't do all the treble clefs at once.)

Does it sound too easy? It is—if you weren't timing yourself. But don't do this at a comfortable pace. Do it as fast as you can. See how many seconds it takes to complete each grid the first time. Then pause for a few minutes and do something else entirely. Eat an apple, feed the fish, or polish the plants. Then complete the same grid again, trying to beat your first time. Then pause again, and try even harder the third time.

You'll notice that our abbreviations for the musical symbols are obvious and aren't meant to slow you down. (For example, the abbreviation for "treble clef" is TC. Under the treble clef symbol, write "TC.") You're exercising your "mental reflexes," not your memory, and the whole point here is speed.

Key: 𝄞 = treble clef (TC)   c = 4/4 (common) time (CT)

       𝄢 = bass clef (BC)   ¢ = 2/2 (half) time (HT)

Key: ♯ = sharp (SH)   ✕ = double sharp (DS)

       ♭ = flat (FL)   ♭♭ = double flat (DF)

Speed

What we're exercising here is the mental equivalent of eye-hand coordination. Think of it as "eye-brain" coordination. In the first half of the chapter, we're concentrating on speed. Just as your quick reflexes can help you save a vase that is teetering precariously on the edge of a table, they can help you recognize the right sign on an unfamiliar highway *before* you pass the exit instead of afterward.

My assistant was recently in the park with a friend, watching all the dogs tussling with each other and dancing around the dog run. Unexpectedly, they heard a rustling sound in the trees above, and saw a hapless squirrel heading for ground zero behind enemy lines—and without a parachute, yet. Hitting the ground unceremoniously, the squirrel blinked his eyes to discover a dozen dogs all eyeing him with great interest, but before you could say "Rin-Tin-Tin," he shot off at warp speed, somehow finding the straight line through that one small hole in the fence. Can we do as well? Yes. (Just ask any air-traffic controller or fighter pilot.)

This is the sort of thing that mental organization can help to accomplish, and there are plenty of ways to exercise it. Take any "mental sport"—SCRABBLE™, checkers, or chess—and play it at high speed. Have you ever watched a game of "speed chess"? My son is an international master, and when he played speed chess as an exercise for tournaments, he and his opponents made the moves at a lightning pace, setting the clock accordingly.

Start increasing your speed fairly slowly. That is, begin by taking your time, but set a reasonable limit. If you like chess, set your computer to a comfortable level or play with a partner who has equivalent expertise. (In my own case, I'll need to find someone who refers to the knights as "horsies.") As you learn to move faster, turn up the speed. (In chess, this will actually decrease the level of difficulty. When the computer takes longer to "think," it makes better moves.) You won't play better, but playing better isn't the point. Instead, the point is to play as well as you can— but faster. (In speed chess, the moves cannot be analyzed as fully as in regular chess, but most of the top players still use it as a mental exercise.)

You don't have to use chess, of course. Maybe checkers is the game for you, or SCRABBLE™. Whatever you choose, start to set a time limit to your moves. Be generous at first. Then, after a week or two, reduce the time. Wait a week and reduce it again. After a month or two, both you and your partner will surprise unprepared onlookers with your newfound mental agility.

Another good exercise is jigsaw-puzzle competition. (I used to do this with my son and daughter myself, and we spent quite a few snowy winter evenings happily snapping pieces into place.) To increase your speed, arrange it so that you and your partner (or partners) each have an identical jigsaw puzzle and race to see who can complete his or hers the fastest. It's great fun and turns an ordinary pastime into a much more constructive one for the family.

Here are exercises:

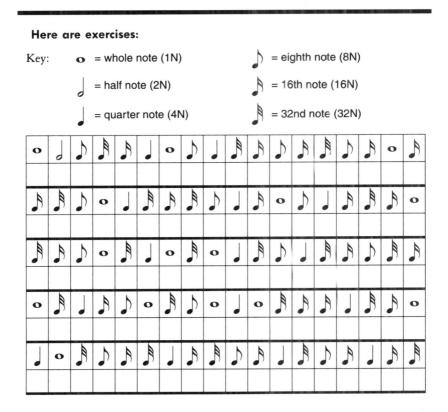

Key: ━ = whole rest (1R)   ɤ = eighth rest (8R)

       ▬ = half rest (2R)   ϟ = 16th rest (16R)

       ₹ = quarter rest (4R)   ϟ = 32nd rest (32R)

Speaking of rests, we'll bet you could use one by now. But we're sure you had a good workout, and that's what's important.

Being able to access and process information readily can be of great significance to success in life. No one is going to be interested in whether you can use Schrödinger's wave equation rapidly (or effectively, for that matter), but if you're not mentally "quick" with the numbers in your field, you'll be outwitted easily, by competing co-workers, by clients, and by the competition. Worse, you won't be able to make correct decisions without very carefully figuring everything out on paper first. That's fine for major projects, but it's crippling for the minor ones.

Remember, we're not suggesting that you speed up your pace and expend more energy in life. Rapid understanding actually takes *less* effort than slow understanding, and it frees time for anything else you want to do—whether it's work, play, or brushing the cat.

In addition, a quick mind inspires confidence, and deservedly so. Would the U.S.S. *Enterprise* have outwitted the Klingons so many times if Captain Kirk had usually said, "Ah . . . hmm . . . well, maybe we should have a meeting about this"? Of course not, or he wouldn't have been the captain for long. Whether you're the chief executive officer of your company, a single parent struggling to pay the bills, or a starship captain, you need all the help you can get, and a quick mind helps.

Mental
Organization

Accuracy

How accurate are your "mental reflexes"?

1. Sometimes I run into people I know at the theater or grocery store, but I haven't a clue as to what their names are!
2. I'm one of those people who hangs up on answering machines because I seem incapable of leaving a message that doesn't sound silly.
3. I come up with an answer fairly quickly on multiple-choice tests, but then I often change it. And then I learn that I was right the *first* time.
4. I've always been pretty good at math and spelling bees.
5. "I can name that tune in two notes . . ."

A "true" to number 1 is normal, but a "true" to number 2 is not, although it's fairly common. Stay tuned—we'll bring it up again later. And a "true" to number 3? It's common, but not a problem. Most conventional wisdom says that when your answer is a guess, don't go back and change it. 'False" to number 4? Well, join the club, but don't worry about it—these "bees" are meant to be tricky, so they're not representative of a problem. And a "true" to number 5? You've been paging ahead, haven't you?

Here are more exercises, but the instructions for this half of the chapter are somewhat different:

Following are the same common musical symbols we looked at before, accompanied by their names and our abbreviations for them. Below each group is a blank exercise grid. Again, make photocopies of each page and complete every grid at least twice.

Here's how to complete the grids this time: First you'll find a "key" that shows the symbols. Study it for a few moments. Then, again referring to the key as often as you like, draw the correct symbol below each abbreviation in the exercise grid, moving from left to right, the way you usually write. (And yes, you shouldn't do all the treble clefs at once.)

Time yourself again, but don't do the exercise quite as fast as you can. Instead, do it only as fast as you can draw the symbols with good accuracy. (Don't be a perfectionist, though; André Previn will not be conducting from your grid.) Note how many seconds it takes to complete each grid the first time, and then pause for a few minutes again the way you did before. Polish an apple, eat the fish, or feed the plants. Then complete the same grid again, trying to beat your first time, but without sacrificing accuracy. Pause again, and try harder the third time.

The symbols are the same (and so are the abbreviations, of course), so you should be familiar with them by now. (Under the "TC" abbreviation, you should draw a treble clef.) And don't forget that accuracy is as important as speed.

Key: treble clef (TC) = 𝄞   4/4 (or common) time (CT) = c

         bass clef (BC) = 𝄢   2/2 (or half) time (HT) = ¢

HT	TC	BC	CT	TC	BC	CT	TC	BC	HT	CT	TC	HT	BC	HT	TC	CT	HT
CT	HT	CT	TC	CT	BC	TC	HT	CT	HT	BC	TC	HT	TC	BC	HT	TC	CT
TC	HT	BC	CT	TC	HT	BC	HT	CT	TC	HT	BC	CT	HT	CT	BC	HT	BC
TC	CT	HT	TC	BC	CT	TC	CT	BC	HT	TC	CT	BC	HT	TC	CT	BC	HT
HT	TC	BC	CT	TC	BC	CT	HT	TC	BC	CT	HT	BC	TC	CT	HT	TC	CT

Key: sharp (SH) = ♯   double sharp (CS) = 𝄪

         flat (FL) = ♭   double flat (DF) = ♭♭

DF	FL	SH	DF	CS	DF	SH	FL	DF	CS	SH	FL	DF	CS	SH	FL	CS	SH
CS	SH	FL	DF	FL	CS	SH	FL	DF	FL	SH	CS	DF	FL	CS	FL	SH	FL
DF	CS	SH	FL	CS	SH	DF	CS	FL	DF	CS	SH	CS	SH	FL	DF	SH	CS
DF	FL	SH	DF	FL	DF	CS	SH	FL	DF	FL	DF	FL	SH	CS	FL	DF	FL
SH	FL	DF	SH	DF	FL	CS	DF	CS	FL	DF	SH	CS	FL	DF	SH	DF	CS

Accuracy

You're intelligent. We know that. And how do we know it? Because you're reading this book. No, don't laugh! The people who are most interested in strengthening their intelligence are usually quite intelligent already. (People who join gyms are not usually overweight and/or out of shape. They look pretty good when they walk in the door and want to look even better in the future.) The point of this chapter, then, is to encourage a more spontaneous flow of the intelligence you already have.

One good way to learn how to think on your feet is to get involved in public speaking, but that terrorizes a great many people, so we won't suggest it at first. (We know, we know. Just thinking about it makes your socks roll up and down.) But you can start small. Think of a subject about which you're knowledgeable. You're a claims adjuster? Make it insurance. You're an artist? Make it pigment. You're a gourmet cook? Make it wine. Then, get out your tape recorder, and when no one else is around, tell it everything you know about the subject in thirty minutes (but no more) and without preparation. Listen to the tape. How did you do? Was your performance organized, informative, and did it cover the topic adequately? Or did you just babble on like a brook? Or did you have trouble thinking of things to say? If you did, you clearly need more practice in mental organization, because you couldn't have run out of things to say about a favorite subject in only thirty minutes. Try it several more times and listen to yourself.

Also try doing the same thing with popular subjects like "television" or "film." Maybe you could even narrate a thirty-minute discussion of a favorite book. Then, after you've practiced this for a while, begin to leave longer, more complete messages on answering machines—but don't think about what you're going to say ahead of time. Spontaneous mental organization is the goal, not memorization.

Did you ever wonder how stage actors can possibly manage to memorize an entire play? Well, they don't, really. Instead, their lines arise within the context of the action. That is, given the situation on stage at the moment, including previous lines, if the actor has successfully "become" the character, he knows what the character would logically say next. (We know this is an oversimplification, and we realize that acting is an art form, but it's also a good example of how mental organization differs from memorization.)

Reading a book about a subject and then telling a friend all about it can be good exercise, fun, and even educational. Say you've decided to learn all there is to know about the subject of corn, and you buy a book about its history. (You think we're kidding, don't you? Nope. Us? Kid you? There actually is a fairly recent book called, unbelievably, *The Story of Corn.*) Then bring up the subject when you're out with friends (but make sure they're close friends, or you'll scare them). And if you can make the subject of corn as interesting to them as it is to you, let us know. We want to sign up for public-speaking lessons with you.

Back to the last of the exercises:

Key: whole note (1N) = o   eighth note (8N) = ♪

half note (2N) = ♩   16th note (16N) = ♬

quarter note (4N) = ♩   32nd note (32N) = ♬

4N	2N	1N	32N	2N	8N	4N	2N	16N	1N	4N	2N	1N	8N	2N	1N	8N	32N
32N	4N	32N	8N	4N	32N	1N	2N	16N	8N	16N	2N	4N	1N	8N	2N	16N	1N
1N	16N	8N	4N	1N	32N	2N	16N	2N	4N	1N	32N	8N	4N	1N	8N	16N	32N
16N	1N	8N	2N	4N	16N	32N	2N	1N	4N	2N	1N	8N	4N	1N	8N	16N	32N
32N	2N	1N	16N	8N	1N	4N	32N	2N	16N	4N	1N	8N	2N	4N	16N	1N	8N

Key: whole rest (1R) = ▬   eighth rest (8R) = 𝄾

           half rest (2R) = ▬   16th rest (16R) = 𝄿

           quarter rest (4R) = 𝄽   32nd rest (32R) = 𝅀

1R	2R	4R	16R	8R	32R	4R	1R	4R	8R	2R	16R	1R	4R	8R	2R	16R	32R

1R	32R	4R	16R	2R	1R	8R	32R	4R	1R	8R	2R	16R	32R	4R	8R	2R	16R

16R	4R	1R	2R	8R	16R	4R	1R	2R	8R	1R	32R	1R	4R	2R	8R	16R	32R

32R	1R	2R	8R	1R	4R	16R	8R	2R	4R	1R	16R	8R	2R	4R	1R	32R	16R

32R	8R	1R	2R	4R	16R	1R	8R	2R	4R	16R	8R	2R	1R	16R	32R	4R	32R

Strong mental organization gives you fast and easy access to the most important things you've learned the way an organized desk or kitchen gives you access to what you need, when you need it. And the ability to process information rapidly and accurately makes you enormously more valuable—not just to your employer, but to your friends as well—by lending new meaning to the term "understanding." Mental organization refers not to speed alone and not to accuracy alone, but to the speed *of* accuracy.

Tests of "mental organization" are routinely administered as part of standard intelligence and/or aptitude testing, as are most, often all, of the other skills we've been exercising in this book. In the testing field, memory tests are often called "Sentence Memory," "Passage Memory," and "Digit Memory." General literacy tests are called "General Information," while vocabulary tests are called just that. Writing tests are called "Sentence Completion" and "Sentence Building." General comprehension tests go by that same name, but include "Finding Reasons," as well. Tests of reasoning, ingenuity, codes, picture-completion, similarities and differences, and analogies are also standard. Sequence-arrangement tests are called "Picture Arrangement." Tests of spatial ability and orientation are standard, too. Design-and-assembly tests are called "Block Design" and "Object Assembly," and mental-organization tests are called "Digit Symbol" tests. The only routine tests we didn't cover are "Proverbs" and "Paper-Cutting." And aren't you glad?

You've reached the end of *"I've Forgotten Everything I Learned In School!"* and, hopefully, that comment is no longer appropriate. But don't let this be the end of your effort to regain your education. Our suggestion for you is that you skim back through the book for a subject that especially interests you, and we know you'll find more than one. After all, one or more of the subjects you learned in school may have led you to your career or your hobbies. Have your interests changed over the years? Is there a particular subject that you wished you had studied but didn't know where to start? Well, here's your chance. We worked with important concepts in psychology, English literature, economics, philosophy, human biology, mathematics, physical sciences, film, classical art, comparative religion, political science, U.S. and world history, plane geometry, global geography, English poetry, and music composition. Intellectually speaking, you are a different person now than when you first began to read and work with this book. You learned some things that you never knew before, a few things that you wish you'd known earlier, a couple of things that utterly contradicted what you had taken for granted, and, of course, many things that you knew once but had forgotten. It's been quite an education, hasn't it?

But this book wasn't written to be an end in itself. (Nor was it supposed to be an ironclad regimen. If you did every exercise religiously, fine. If you skipped over some of them, changed the rules here and there, or did others twice, that's fine, too. How often have you been able to tailor your education to suit your own particular needs? After all, you know yourself best. In this case, the end is what counts, not the means.) Instead, this book was written to be a beginning. It could just as easily have been titled *"I've Forgotten Everything I **Wanted** to Learn In School!"*

So start with any of the subjects we've covered, and take off on your own. As Shakespeare *didn't* say, "Get thee to a library." (Or was it a bookstore?) Education at its best is a joyful discovery process, and serendipity can be the most charming of teachers.

About the Author

Marilyn vos Savant was born in St. Louis, Missouri, the daughter of Mary vos Savant and Joseph Mach. She is married to Robert Jarvik, M.D., inventor of the Jarvik-7 artificial heart. They live in New York.

She was listed in the *Guinness Book of World Records* for five years under "Highest I.Q.," for both childhood and adult scores, and has now been inducted into the Guinness Hall of Fame. She is a writer and lecturer, and spends additional time assisting her husband in the artificial-heart program. Her special interests and concerns are quality education and thinking in America, and humanitarian medicine and research. She describes herself as an "independent" with regard to politics and religion, and only an "armchair" feminist.

Marilyn vos Savant writes the "Ask Marilyn" question-and-answer problem-analysis column for *Parade,* the Sunday magazine for 353 newspapers, which has a circulation of thirty-six million and a readership of seventy million, the largest in the world. Her book *Number Blindness* will be published in hardcover in 1995; *More Marilyn,* a second collection of the best questions and answers from the column, will be published in hardcover in September of 1994; *The World's Most Famous Math Problem: The Proof of Fermat's Last Theorem and Other Mathematical Mysteries* trade paperback was published in 1993; and *Ask Marilyn,* the first collection of questions and answers from her column, was published in hardcover in 1992, all by St. Martin's Press.

It Was Poppa's Will, a stage play that vos Savant wrote, was produced in a staged reading, and she has also written a fantasy/ satire (novel) of a dozen classical civilizations in history called *The Re-Creation* and a futuristic political fantasy/satire (novel), as yet untitled.

But vos Savant is far from the stereotype of the intellectual, saying that she believes "an ounce of sequins is worth a pound of home cooking," and that she doesn't engage in the latter "for humanitarian reasons." And what does she do for fun? Read a book? Retreat to the wilderness? She looks surprised. "Not at all," she says. "My idea of fun is going out with people. A park is a nice place to visit, but I wouldn't want to live there. I'd rather be surrounded by a thousand people than a thousand trees." Her hobby is writing letters to friends around the world.